CELE[illegible] YEARS

New York City Dating (and Dumping) Guide

Restaurants, Bars and Other Hot Spots

Published and distributed by
Zagat Survey, LLC
4 Columbus Circle
New York, NY 10019
T: 212.977.6000
www.zagat.com

ACKNOWLEDGMENTS

We thank Leigh Crandall, Alexis DeLaRosa, Mikola De Roo, Jonathan Durbin, Jeremiah Furr, Randi Gollin, Lynn Hazlewood, Carolyn Koo, Nathan Lacy, Nancy Lambert, Scott Laughlin, Julie Mehta, Bernard Onken, Mary Phillips-Sandy, Joanna Prisco, Brian Rattiner, Laura Siciliano-Rosen, Carla Spartos, Brendan Spiegel, Gabby Stein, Kelly Stewart, Rachel Syme, Martin Tyrrell, Miranda Van Gelder, Caren Weiner Campbell and Steve Weinstein, as well as the following members of our staff: Brian Albert, Sean Beachell, Maryanne Bertollo, Jane Chang, Sandy Cheng, Reni Chin, Larry Cohn, Bill Corsello, John Deiner, Carol Diuguid, Caitlin Eichelberger, Alison Flick, Jeff Freier, Shelley Gallagher, Curt Gathje, Sharon Gintzler, Michelle Golden, Justin Hartung, Karen Hudes, Roy Jacob, Garth Johnston, Ashunta Joseph, Cindy Kilian, Natalie Lebert, Mike Liao, Christina Livadiotis, Dave Makulec, Andre Pilette, Josh Rogers, Kimberly Rosado, Becky Ruthenburg, Troy Segal, Aleksandra Shander, Stacey Slate, Albry Smither, Jacqueline Wasilczyk, Donna Marino Wilkins, Sarah Worthington, Yoji Yamaguchi, Sharon Yates, Anna Zappia, Kyle Zolner and Tami Zonenshine.

The reviews in this guide are based on public opinion surveys. The ratings reflect the average scores given by the survey participants who voted on each establishment. The text is based on quotes from, or paraphrasings of, the surveyors' comments. Phone numbers, addresses and other factual data were correct to the best of our knowledge when published in this guide.

ISBN-13: 978-1-60478-019-2
ISBN-10: 1-60478-019-3
Printed in the
United States of America

Contents

Ratings & Symbols

Ratings **Food, Decor** and **Service** (restaurants) and **Appeal, Decor** and **Service** (nightlife) are rated on the Zagat 0 to 30 scale:

0 - 9	poor to fair
10 - 15	fair to good
16 - 19	good to very good
20 - 25	very good to excellent
26 - 30	extraordinary to perfection
▽	low response | less reliable

Cost For **restaurants,** we show our surveyors' benchmark estimate of the price of a dinner with one drink and tip. Lunch is usually 25 to 30% less. At prix fixe-only places we show the charge for the lowest-priced menu plus 30%. For **nightlife,** we show our surveyors' estimated price of a typical single drink. For places listed without ratings, the price range is as follows:

I	Inexpensive	E	Expensive
M	Moderate	VE	Very Expensive

Comments Surveyors' comments are indicated in quotation marks within reviews.

Symbols

- ◐ serves after 11 PM
- Ⓢ closed on Sunday
- Ⓜ closed on Monday
- ≠ no credit cards accepted

About This Survey

We are pleased to present our first-ever Zagat **New York City Dating (and Dumping) Guide.** Along with restaurant and nightlife reviews - broken down into dating- and (tongue-in-cheek) "dumping"-appropriate categories - this book includes highlights from our special dating survey, in which we asked questions about preferences, priorities, pet peeves and pick-up lines, among other things (pages 6-14).

WHO PARTICIPATED: In addition to the more than 44,000 surveyors who contributed to our NYC restaurant and nightlife surveys, we heard from 2,029 opinionated daters. Of these, 64% are women and 36% men. Among the women, 94% are interested in men; 3% in women; and 3% in both. As for the men, 86% are interested in women; 12% in men; and 2% in both. Age-wise, 25% are in their 20s; 36%, 30s; 22%, 40s; 13%, 50s; and 4%, 60s or above. Meanwhile, 18% are married; 27% are dating and consider themselves in relationships; 53% are single and open to meeting someone; and 2% are single and not interested in dating.

ABOUT ZAGAT: This marks our 30th year surveying consumers about their experiences. What started in 1979 as a hobby has come a long way. Today we have over 350,000 surveyors and cover dining, nightlife, entertaining, golf, hotels and more.

INTERACTIVE: Up-to-the-minute news about restaurant openings plus menus, photos and more are free on **ZAGAT.com** and the award-winning **ZAGAT.mobi** (for web-enabled mobile devices). They will enable you to reserve at thousands of places with just one click.

VOTE AND COMMENT: We invite you to join any of our surveys at **ZAGAT.com.** In exchange for doing so, you'll receive a free copy of the resulting guide when published.

AVAILABILITY: Zagat guides are available in all major bookstores as well as on **ZAGAT.com.** You can also access our content when on the go via **ZAGAT.mobi** and **ZAGAT TO GO** (for smartphones).

New York, NY
January 8, 2009

Nina and Tim Zagat

Dating by Numbers

It seems that people have strong feelings about dating and all that goes with it. From "who to date?" to "who should pay?" our opinionated dating public told us what they really think. Here, some of the pleasing and painful highlights:

THE POLITICS OF DATING

In New York City our surveyors are more likely to date outside their race, religion, age group, income bracket, education level and nationality than outside their political party. Democrats and Republicans simply can't get together, not even to give each other lip. Just as important as political affiliation is location: 54% of our respondents would not date someone outside the NYC metro area.

TRUST ISSUES, ANYONE?

When we asked our surveyors if they'd ever snoop into their sweetheart's e-mail/voicemail, bank statement/tax returns, purse/briefcase, dresser drawers or diary/journal given a "reasonable" chance of getting caught, the vast majority said "NO." However, when we take away the chance of being found out, would they do it? "Hell yes," they said. Okay, that's not exactly true, but percentages did jump from just 2.6% who'd read their partner's diary/journal if there was a chance of being caught to 31.4% if there were absolutely no chance of being nabbed.

Dating by Numbers

Love and the Libido

When is the right time for a relationship to become physical? For the vast majority of our surveyors, going on a set number of dates, saying "I love you," even getting married aren't what matter. Rather, 88% believe a relationship should become intimate "whenever it feels right."

Business or Pleasure?

Although it may go against some company policies - and even the law - 10% of our surveyors said they've had luck meeting dates at the office. In fact, 75% of New Yorkers have no problem dating a co-worker, 17% feel comfortable dating their boss and 18% are okay with dating a direct report. Fortunately, our co-founders, Tim and Nina Zagat, were married before they started working together.

The Quickest Way to the Heart Is Through the Stomach

During the quest for true love, dining and dating go hand-in-hand. Nearly 40% of our respondents said a restaurant was the ideal first-date setting, and dinner was the most popular meal for a first date (78%). Apparently the city may sleep after all, because only 1% of New Yorkers would choose breakfast for a first date. When choosing a restaurant for that first get-together, 46% of New Yorkers feel food is the most important consideration, while 41% say decor takes precedence.

Looking for a Date?

Whether you're looking for love at a bar, a coffee shop or even online, you only get one chance to make a first impression. The following pick-up lines, smooth moves and not-so-smooth moves come directly from our surveyors.

Play-It-Safe Approach

These tips and pick-up lines may not be terribly original, but chances are you won't get slapped, and you may just end up with a date...

"Just say hi and make eye contact."
"Start talking about something topical."
"Show you're confident and can hold a good conversation."
"Be real, at ease in your skin and willing to laugh at yourself."
"No games, no b.s."

Here, a few openers our surveyors suggest:

"Hi, how are you?"
"Interesting bracelet - there must be a story behind that."
"You look like you are so happy, I need to know you."
"I will take you anywhere you want tomorrow night, you name it."
"Would you like to go out sometime?"
"Can I buy you a drink?"

Looking for a Date?

Play-It-Stupid Approach

Use any of the lines below and chances are you'll be screwed (and not in a good way...)

"I'd like to introduce you to my future ex-wife."
"You look like something out of a Merchant-Ivory film."
"I like your dress - it would look good on my floor."
"If I wasn't on Prozac, I wouldn't be able to talk to a pretty girl like you."
"I don't care if you're married - so am I!"
"Let me do you a favor and go home with you tonight."
"I dig older ladies like you."
"Wanna f---?"
"My mother would love you."
"You remind me of my sister."
"This is our only chance to have anonymous sex."
"Are you *happily* married?"
"Have we slept together yet?"
"You and I would have really good-looking children."
"Screw me if I'm wrong, but haven't we met before?"
"I just got back from Mexico and picked up some ruffies. Can I buy you a drink?"
"I've just moved you to the top of my 'to do' list."

Sweet Stories

The most common responses to our "most romantic thing" query involved homemade dinners, flowers and marriage proposals. Here, some more unique gestures that would sweep anyone off their feet...

"Offered me the moon and the stars if I would go out with him - and then took me to the observatory."

"Commissioned Sophie Crumb, the daughter of R. Crumb, to ink a comic strip based on my life."

"Warmed socks in the oven for my cold winter feet."

"Tracked down a photograph that was taken of me by a famous photographer many years before, bought the original and had it framed for me."

"Named the main character's love interest after me in one of his books."

"Cleaned my shoe after I stepped in dog #*%+!"

"Gave me a book with my name in the title."

Sweet "Jesus Get Me Out of Here" Stories

As much as we love to hear dating success stories, we can't help but laugh (and cringe) at the worst tales of dating woe. Here are some of our favorites, straight from surveyors...

"When I opted out of a second date, he told me he hoped I died in a fiery car crash."

"Somebody asked me 'Where is this going?' on the first date."

"We were fooling around. I went to use his bathroom, and when I came back he was at his computer checking out online dates."

"The time my date got the waiter's number in front of me."

"I went out with a guy who told me over dinner that he set his parents' house on fire and it burned to the ground."

"The guy who talked with his mouth full, spewing food at my face - I needed an umbrella."

Sweet "Jesus Get Me Out of Here" Stories (continued)

"My date was drunk minutes after arriving at the restaurant and then condoms spilled out of her purse like a waterfall."

"My long-distance boyfriend came to pick me up at the airport... with his new girlfriend."

"All he could talk about was who he'd slept with, what he liked to do in bed, how cold all the women were who didn't want to sleep with him and how long it would take me to sleep with him..."

"In the middle of an intimate moment, my so-called boyfriend said 'I don't think I can do this anymore because I'm engaged.'"

"I was attempting to run my fingers through my date's hair when my fingers became tangled in his hairpiece."

"He told me that his fetish was amputees and if something were to happen to me I would be right up there at the top of his list."

"A guy fell asleep at the table across from me during our first date."

"I thought he was going to take me out to dinner, but he explained that he doesn't like to eat and only eats to survive, so we weren't going out to eat."

"The guy would not stop talking about himself - his travels, his brilliant mind. By the end of the night he was trying to get me to give him made-up math problems to solve so he could prove his genius."

"I went out with someone who told me about his anger management counseling and followed up with a story of how he tried to rip someone out of his car through the window for cutting him off on his bike."

"I went out with a model. He brought his portfolio and broke down every photo of himself. He could see the boredom on my face and said that if I wasn't interested I should leave but if I was, he'd be willing to have sex with me."

Pet Peeves & Deal-Breakers

Issues With Men

These women would rather be single than sorry, especially if the guy...

- Has the "shopping mentality": likes the woman he's with but is always looking for the next one
- Spends more time getting ready than she does
- Stares inappropriately at her body parts
- Lies about his age
- Doesn't open the door for her
- Constantly talks about other women and exes
- Has mommy issues
- Expects some action at the end of the night

Issues With Women

These men would rather be a bachelor than a boyfriend if the woman...

- Talks to cats
- Wants to do an IRS audit on his income
- Is not clear on her sexuality
- Expects to be courted excessively
- Acts like a princess, craving attention, drama or money
- Doesn't wait for him to open the door
- Wears old-lady clothes
- Wears too much perfume on a first date

"Totally Reasonable" Grounds for Dismissal

There's a good chance these surveyors will be single for a long time, since they'll stop seeing someone who...

- Chooses Mexican food for the first date
- Gratuitously uses exclamation points in email
- Is a carnivore
- Can only commit to meet for a cup of coffee on a first date
- Has incompatible pheromones
- Has bad taste in music
- Cannot spell or use proper grammar
- Has a mother who's not either dead or far, far away
- Has never left the country
- Expects to automatically enter into an exclusive relationship
- Uses foreign words when it's not necessary (think "vino")

#1 Online Dating Complaint

- Meeting someone whose pictures are strikingly unrelated to reality

Pet Peeves & Deal-Breakers

Reasons Money Sometimes Can Buy You Love

When it comes to the bill, men can't stand it when women...

- Never dip into their own pocket (or even make a gratuitous wallet grab)
- Expect the man to pay for the woman's friend (if she's accompanied by a friend)
- Order the most expensive items on the menu

And women can't stand it when men...

- Don't offer to pay on the first date
- Don't bring cash
- Want to go Dutch right down to the cent during the first few dates

Dining Don'ts

In the world of dating, bad dining habits won't get you far. Our surveyors can't deal with a date who...

- Chews with his/her mouth open
- Picks a nice restaurant and complains about how expensive it is
- Texts during dinner or sets a Blackberry on the table
- Is impatient and cruel to waiters
- Tells you what to order or, even worse, orders for you
- Is a picky eater or thinks all food tastes the same
- Does not say thank you when the other person pays

Turn-Offs

It may be over if your date:

- Has multiple piercings
- Shows signs of clinginess/neediness
- Is addicted to smoking
- Lives with mom and dad
- Yawns while you're talking
- Absolutely doesn't want kids
- Gives you a nickname after meeting for the first time

It will definitely be over if your date:

- Doesn't let you get a word in
- Is always negative, has a bad attitude and likes to complain
- Is bigoted/homophobic/racist/sexist
- Checks out other people during your date
- Calls you "baby," "babe" or any derivative thereof
- Refuses to tell you what they do for a living
- Doesn't like kissing

East Coast vs. West Coast

Weather and availability of personal living space aren't the only things that separate NYers from their Southern California counterparts. We discovered definite differences of opinion when we broke down who said what - and where.

Bartender vs. Barista

New Yorkers and Los Angelenos agree that bars are the second most popular setting for a first date, though consensus breaks down when it comes to poison preference. New Yorkers feel a traditional bar (one that includes a bouncer and booze) is the best setting for that early get-together. Angelenos, on the other hand, prefer coffee bars to the kind that serve Red Bull and vodka. Rest assured, all agree that some kind of legal drug, be it alcohol or caffeine, is crucial to a first date.

Dating Deep vs. Dating Shallow

New Yorkers want brains and beauty while Los Angelenos just want to laugh. New Yorkers agree the #1 characteristic they look for in a partner is intelligence. Los Angelenos first want someone with personality and a great sense of humor (and who cares if they don't know why they're laughing?). Overall character was also important to Angelenos, while New Yorkers are more concerned with a partner's attractiveness (at least they'll look good while they're stealing your wallet).

Picking Up the Tab vs. Faux Wallet Grab?

Dealing with the bill is almost as awkward as trying to avoid a kiss at the end of a bad first date. Sixty percent of New Yorkers feel the man should always pay for the first outing, while the majority of our surveyors in Los Angeles believe the person who extended the invitation should foot the bill. If everyone followed these guidelines, maybe there wouldn't be so much confusion. Or maybe a round of credit card roulette would settle the issue.

WHERE TO DATE

	FOOD	DECOR	SERVICE	COST

Restaurants

BRUNCH SPOTS

For the morning after the night before

	FOOD	DECOR	SERVICE	COST
Balthazar ◐ *French*	23	23	19	$55

SoHo | 80 Spring St. (bet. B'way & Crosby St.) | 212-965-1414 | www.balthazarny.com

"More juggernaut than restaurant", Keith McNally's "action-packed" SoHo "beehive" offers "toothsome" French food, "deft" service and a "pitch-perfect" rendering of a Parisian brasserie; expect lots of "hubbub", "tough reservations", moderately "pricey" tabs and a "loud" crowd that runs the gamut from "skeletal models" and fat cats to "celebs" and starstruck "tourists"; in sum, it's *presque* Paris.

	FOOD	DECOR	SERVICE	COST
Blue Ribbon Bakery ◐ *American*	24	18	20	$41

G Village | 35 Downing St. (Bedford St.) | 212-337-0404 | www.blueribbonrestaurants.com

"Amazing smells" issue from this "classic" Village New American from the Bromberg brothers, where a "working bakery" and a "bustling bistro" put out "fresh-baked bread" and "down-home delicious" meals; sure, it can be "noisy and crowded", but it's ever a "standout" for "terrific" brunching - "if you can get a seat."

	FOOD	DECOR	SERVICE	COST
elmo ◐ *American*	16	18	16	$34

Chelsea | 156 Seventh Ave. (bet. 19th & 20th Sts.) | 212-337-8000 | www.elmorestaurant.com

This "lively", "loungey" Chelsea New American may serve only "average" eats but still lures a "beefcake" crowd with its "*Sex and the Gay City*" vibe; "cute waif" waiters and "affordable" tabs help make it a "local go-to" and a brunch "favorite."

	FOOD	DECOR	SERVICE	COST
Five Points ◐ *American/Mediterranean*	22	21	21	$49

NoHo | 31 Great Jones St. (bet. Bowery & Lafayette St.) | 212-253-5700 | www.fivepointsrestaurant.com

"Popular" with "hipster" locals, this NoHo Med-New American plies "inspired" seasonal dishes and "spot-on" service in a "pretty room" with a "bubbling brook" running through it; "noise level" aside, it's a "treat" that scores extra points with its "what-a-scene brunch."

Isabella's *American/Mediterranean* 20 | 19 | 19 | $43

W 70s | 359 Columbus Ave. (77th St.) | 212-724-2100 | www.brguestrestaurants.com

Ever "bustling", this longtime Upper West Side "default" from Steve Hanson is "always crowded" thanks to "delicious", well-priced Mediterranean-New American fare with "something to please everyone"; "pleasant" service and a "mainstay brunch" add to its appeal, along with "revered sidewalk seating" perfect for Columbus Avenue "people-watching."

Jane *American* 21 | 17 | 19 | $40

G Village | 100 W. Houston St. (bet. La Guardia Pl. & Thompson St.) | 212-254-7000

"Popular for good reason", this Greenwich Village "find" offers an "imaginative", "moderately priced" New American menu with "enough variety to please everyone"; throw in "personable" service and a "relaxed" ambiance, and it's no surprise the "killer" brunch is such a "scene."

Nice Matin ◐ *French/Mediterranean* 19 | 18 | 17 | $46

W 70s | 201 W. 79th St. (Amsterdam Ave.) | 212-873-6423 | www.nicematinnyc.com

"Lively and likable", this Upper West Side "asset" attracts the "trendies" with a "moderately priced" French-Mediterranean menu and a "convivial" bistro setting modeled on the "Côte d'Azur"; extras include "outside seating" and a "solid brunch", but beware of the sometimes "amateurish service."

CHEF'S TABLES

The ultimate intimate dining experience

Barbuto *Italian* 21 | 17 | 17 | $51

W Village | 775 Washington St. (bet. Jane & W. 12th Sts.) | 212-924-9700 | www.barbutonyc.com

Set in a revamped garage, Jonathan Waxman's "industro-chic" West Village Italian is "best in summertime" when the "doors are open", but all year round you'll find "market-fresh" meals "simply but stunningly prepared" for an "affordable" cost; but even though the eats are up to speed, some say the "absentminded" staff could use a tune-up.

	FOOD	DECOR	SERVICE	COST
Hearth *American/Italian*	25	20	23	$65

E Village | 403 E. 12th St. (1st Ave.) | 646-602-1300 | www.restauranthearth.com

"Casual yet sophisticated", Marco Canora's "adult" East Villager is "everything dining should be" thanks to "uniquely subtle" Tuscan-American cooking served by an "enthusiastic staff" in "warm" digs (the best seats are at the counter overlooking the open kitchen's "wood-burning oven"); granted, it's "expensive", but the overall "fantastic experience" is well "worth the price."

	FOOD	DECOR	SERVICE	COST
Il Buco ◐ *Italian/Mediterranean*	24	22	21	$61

NoHo | 47 Bond St. (bet. Bowery & Lafayette St.) | 212-533-1932 | www.ilbuco.com

"Sophisticated" meets "earthy" on the "magic" menu of this "original" NoHo Med-Italian where a "beautiful", "bubbly" crowd is "transported" by an antiques-laden "farmhouse setting" (and "romantic" wine cellar); throw in "superb service" and the "big prices" are easy to swallow.

	FOOD	DECOR	SERVICE	COST
Mercat *Spanish*	22	20	18	$51

NoHo | 45 Bond St. (bet. Bowery & Lafayette St.) | 212-529-8600 | www.mercatnyc.com

"Hot from day one", this "like-in-Barcelona" NoHo tapas bar showcases "authentic" Catalan cooking in a "hip", "noisy" setting complete with "open kitchen"; it's a prime "date place" that's also "fun for groups", though service can be "slow" and "tabs mount quickly."

	FOOD	DECOR	SERVICE	COST
Resto ◐ *Belgian*	20	15	17	$42

Gramercy | 111 E. 29th St. (bet. Lexington Ave. & Park Ave. S.) | 212-685-5585 | www.restonyc.com

"Delights" including "top-notch burgers" and one of "NYC's best beer menus" produce "traffic jams" at this "small", "stark" Gramercy Belgian; for most it's "worth" the "painful wait" to get in, but a skeptical few opine it's "overhyped" and too "noisy" to provide much of a resto.

	FOOD	DECOR	SERVICE	COST
Talay ◐ *Pan-Latin/Thai*	-	-	-	M

Harlem | 701 W. 135th St. (12th Ave.) | 212-491-8300 | www.talayrestaurant.com

Uptown hipsters mingle over cocktails and Thai-Latino small plates at this arrival to a happening stretch of Harlem's 12th Avenue that some have dubbed 'ViVa' (that's short for 'Viaduct Valley'); from the dragon statues at its entrance to the sleek bar, upstairs lounge and cavernous, dimly lit dining room, it's all about seeing and being seen - if not being heard.

Yuva *Indian* ∇ 22 | 17 | 19 | $46

E 50s | 230 E. 58th St. (bet. 2nd & 3rd Aves.) | 212-339-0090 | www.yuvanyc.com

"Sublimely spiced" specialties satisfy subcontinental sympathizers at this "upscale" East Midtown Indian, where the "charming" (if sometimes "slow") staff delivers "authentic" standards in vaguely "corporate" quarters; sealing the deal are relatively "reasonable" prices and a "fantastic" $14 lunch buffet.

COOKING CLASSES

Show that you're willing to get your hands dirty

Bouley, Upstairs *Eclectic* 25 | 16 | 18 | $50

TriBeCa | 130 W. Broadway (Duane St.) | 212-608-5829 | www.davidbouley.com

Have a "bite of Bouley flavor at a fraction of the price" at this TriBeCa Eclectic that will offer more "elbow room" once it expands downstairs from its original second-floor location; maybe the "decor's not the reason to visit", but the "cuisine-crossing" menu (including sushi) is so "creative" you won't care.

CamaJe ◐ *American/French* 22 | 15 | 19 | $37

G Village | 85 MacDougal St. (bet. Bleecker & Houston Sts.) | 212-673-8184 | www.camaje.com

Chef Abigail Hitchcock's "creative" menu supplies a true "foodie experience" for "good value" at this "small" Franco-American that's a "welcome escape from the MacDougal Street madness"; extras include "cooking classes", "wine tastings" and blindfolded "dining-in-the-dark" nights.

Carol's Cafe Ⓢ Ⓜ *Eclectic* 24 | 19 | 21 | $55

Staten Island | 1571 Richmond Rd. (bet. Four Corners Rd. & Seaview Ave.) | 718-979-5600 | www.carolscafe.com

"Haute cuisine" comes to "little old Staten Island" at this "unique" Eclectic where "top-notch" chef Carol Frazzetta displays an "artistic" touch with her "inventive" offerings; though it's a "beautiful dining experience for any borough", prices tend toward "Manhattan."

ECO-FRIENDLY FARE

Because eating green is the new black

applewood Ⓜ *American* — 25 | 20 | 22 | $48

Park Slope | 501 11th St. (bet. 7th & 8th Aves.) | Brooklyn | 718-788-1810 | www.applewoodny.com

"Intensely flavored" New American plates are assembled from organic, sustainably grown ingredients "fresh off the farm" at this "charming", "country inn"-like Park Sloper; "scanty portions" at Manhattan prices are offset by "civilized service", "relaxed" vibrations and an "out-of-this-world" brunch.

Blue Hill *American* — 26 | 22 | 25 | $76

G Village | 75 Washington Pl. (bet. MacDougal St. & 6th Ave.) | 212-539-1776 | www.bluehillfarm.com

"Produce so fresh it hasn't been planted yet" is the secret ingredient of "wizard" Dan Barber's "organic chic" New American, specializing in "exquisite seasonal creations" emphasizing "local artisanal" items; throw in a "tranquil" Village setting, "gracious" service and a "romantic garden", and it's easy to see why this "locavore's dream" is worth the "hedge-fund" pricing.

Broadway East Ⓜ *Vegetarian* — ▽ 21 | 23 | 19 | $45

LES | 171 E. Broadway (bet. Jefferson & Rutgers Sts.) | 212-228-3100 | www.broadwayeast.com

Sustainability gets a stylish twist at this Lower East Side "nouveau vegetarian" set in a "drop-dead-gorgeous" space complete with a plant-sprouting wall; the "delicious" seasonal offerings range from grilled pizzas to macrobiotic plates (and even some fish and poultry), while the green/locavore ethos extends to the local beers and wines on offer.

Cookshop ◐ *American* — 23 | 19 | 21 | $52

Chelsea | 156 10th Ave. (20th St.) | 212-924-4440 | www.cookshopny.com

"Locavores" love the "ever-changing", "market-driven" menu at this "clever" Chelsea American that's designed "with foodies in mind"; sure, prices are "high" and the "hustle and bustle" can get "loud", but a "pleasant" ambiance, "down-to-earth" service and a "diverse" crowd make for "terrific" supping.

Little Giant *American* 23 | 18 | 19 | $45

LES | 85 Orchard St. (Broome St.) | 212-226-5047 | www.littlegiantnyc.com

Sizewise it's "more little than giant", but this "sweet" Lower Eastsider's "deceptively simple" New American cooking based on "fresh", "seasonal" ingredients "makes a big impression"; there are sometimes "waits" and elbow room is scarce, but its "excellent vibe" and "warm" service overcome all.

Marlow & Sons ◐ *French* ∇ 23 | 21 | 19 | $38

Williamsburg | 81 Broadway (bet. Berry St. & Wythe Ave.) | Brooklyn | 718-384-1441 | www.marlowandsons.com

The kitchen is "firing on all cylinders" at this tiny Williamsburg "charmer" and Diner sibling that's part "old-style general store", part bar/eatery plying a "limited" roster of "seasonal" French-influenced bites and "rockin'" wine and cocktails; just bear in mind that you "gotta fight with the local hipmongers" for a seat.

Savoy *American/Mediterranean* 23 | 20 | 22 | $58

SoHo | 70 Prince St. (Crosby St.) | 212-219-8570 | www.savoynyc.com

"Deft" chef Peter Hoffman is the "king of seasonal cooking" declare "locavores" who favor his "SoHo classic" for "fabulous", "farm-fresh" fare delivered by a "well-trained" staff; the "country-home" decor ("sit upstairs for romance") and "superlative" wines secure diners' support.

FIREPLACE SETTINGS

Because everyone looks better by firelight

Aspen ◐ ☒ *American* 18 | 23 | 16 | $48

Flatiron | 30 W. 22nd St. (bet. 5th & 6th Aves.) | 212-645-5040 | www.aspen-nyc.com

"Wear black", "be young" and "drop names" to fit in at this "clublike" Flatiron New American offering "delicious" tapas and "après-work" scenery in a faux "Swiss chalet" setting complete with "roaring log fire"; too bad the "high prices" match the staff's "high attitude."

Park, The ◐ *Mediterranean* 15 | 23 | 14 | $40

Chelsea | 118 10th Ave. (bet. 17th & 18th Sts.) | 212-352-3313 | www.theparknyc.com

Scenesters admire the "amazing space" at this "sprawling" West Chelsea outpost as they gather "by the fireplace" or in the "pretty" garden for "partying" and "people-watching"; but given "underwhelming" Med fare and "lacking service", many "go to look, not to eat."

Place, The *American/Mediterranean* 21 23 20 $47

W Village | 310 W. Fourth St. (bet. Bank & 12th Sts.) | 212-924-2711 | www.theplaceny.com

The "quintessential quaint Village" eatery, this "romantic hideaway" remains a "well-kept secret" despite its "delicious" Med-New American fare and "super-sweet" service; a "cozy" "winter dinner" near its fireplace "warms the heart" - "if you can't sweep a date off his or her feet" here, "you're hopeless."

Public *Eclectic* 22 24 21 $53

NoLita | 210 Elizabeth St. (bet. Prince & Spring Sts.) | 212-343-7011 | www.public-nyc.com

The "elementary-school-chic" decor (card catalogs, "modern industrialist" lighting) sets the "sexy scene" at this NoLita "mainstay"; all can appreciate its "imaginative" "Aussie"-accented Eclectic eats and "killer cocktails", though the "high prices" mean it's "not for all of the public."

South Gate *American* 24 25 22 $81

W 60s | Jumeirah Essex House | 154 Central Park S. (bet. 6th & 7th Aves.) | 212-484-5120 | www.jumeirahessexhouse.com

Chef Kerry Heffernan (ex Eleven Madison Park) brings his "magic" to this Central Park South New American, sending out "exceptional" cuisine in a "modern", "sprawling" space "overlooking Central Park"; "solicitous" service and a "dynamite bar" are two more reasons to come - as long as you can afford it.

GIRLS' NIGHT OUT

Because sometimes friends make the best "dates"

Centro Vinoteca ◐ *Italian* 22 19 19 $51

W Village | 74 Seventh Ave. S. (Barrow St.) | 212-367-7470 | www.centrovinoteca.com

A "trendy", midpriced West Village Italian "scene" where "superb *piccolini*" (small plates) and vino in quartinos encourage sharing; the "cute" servers may "still need some polish" and the "lively" room verges on "deafening", but upstairs is "more subdued"; N.B. the departure of chef Anne Burrell puts its Food Score in question.

'inoteca ◐ *Italian* 23 | 18 | 20 | $39

LES | 98 Rivington St. (Ludlow St.) | 212-614-0473 | www.inotecanyc.com

"Exceptional small plates" and a "cocktail-party" vibe lure "the young and vibrant" to this LES panini-and-vino specialist, where patient staffers "translate the Italian menu"; expect the same "long waits", "high volume" and "decent pricing" as at its sibling, 'ino, but more room.

Josie's *Eclectic* 19 | 15 | 16 | $34

Murray Hill | 565 Third Ave. (37th St.) | 212-490-1558

W 70s | 300 Amsterdam Ave. (74th St.) | 212-769-1212

Josie's Kitchen *Eclectic*

E 80s | 1614 Second Ave. (84th St.) | 212-734-6644

www.josiesnyc.com

"Virtuous", mostly organic grub makes for "sin-free" dining at this well-priced Eclectic trio that's particularly popular with "girls'-night-out" groups; however, "patience is needed" at peak times when the "minimalist" digs get "noisy" and the "frazzled" staff seems to "take forever."

GREAT FOOD, LITTLE KNOWN

Good food as foreplay

Brown Café *American* ▽ 22 | 15 | 20 | $30

LES | 61 Hester St. (bet. Essex & Ludlow Sts.) | 212-477-2427

Exuding a whiff of "downtown bohemia", this "low-tech", under-the-radar LES cafe draws "casual hipsters" with "well-priced" seasonal New Americana; despite "tiny" digs and "uncomfortable", "lumberjack-chic" furnishings, this sleeper remains a "neighborhood" favorite.

La Ripaille *French* ▽ 23 | 20 | 21 | $48

W Village | 605 Hudson St. (bet. Bethune & W. 12th Sts.) | 212-255-4406 | www.laripailleny.com

The owner "really goes out of his way to make you feel welcome" at this "old warhorse" that's the "very definition" of a "warm", "cozy" "Village bistro"; with "honest French cooking" considered "worth every penny", it's a cherished "neighborhood" "standby."

Mancora ◐ *Peruvian* ▽ 22 | 14 | 21 | $28

E Village | 99 First Ave. (6th St.) | 212-253-1011

At this "homey" East Village Peruvian, the "delicious", "value"-oriented specialties ("huge, fresh platters of ceviche", the "best chicken I've had in ages") are "presented with pride"; the decor may be "modest", but it "never fails to welcome."

Rosanjin Ⓢ *Japanese* ▽ 27 | 27 | 26 | $153

TriBeCa | 141 Duane St. (bet. Church St. & W. B'way) | 212-346-0664 | www.rosanjintribeca.com

The kaiseki meals at this "peaceful" TriBeCa Japanese are "formal" multicourse extravaganzas "exquisitely presented" and "served with exceeding courtesy" - in short, an "outstanding", "super-luxurious" experience; all that's required is "time" and deep pockets to cover the $150 prix fixe (though an à la carte menu is now available too).

Ushiwakamaru ◐Ⓢ *Japanese* ▽ 27 | 15 | 20 | $72

G Village | 136 W. Houston St. (bet. MacDougal & Sullivan Sts.) | 212-228-4181

"Aficionados" who know this "small", under-the-radar Village Japanese hail the "master" behind its sushi bar and his "Tokyo-style" preparations of fish "flown in from Japan"; "book a seat at the bar" for the omakase - but beware tabs that quickly "run up."

HISTORIC PLACES

Borrow an air of longevity for your budding relationship

Café des Artistes ◐ *French* 22 | 26 | 23 | $69

W 60s | 1 W. 67th St. (bet. Columbus Ave. & CPW) | 212-877-3500 | www.cafenyc.com

The "older the violin, the sweeter the music" says it all about this "classy" UWS "grande dame" via George and Jenifer Lang that "still seduces" with an "oh-so-romantic setting" that combines "beautiful flowers" and "sensual murals" of wood nymphs with "delicious" French dishes and "excellent service"; a "feast for the eyes and palate", it's "quintessential NYC" and worth every penny.

Commerce *American* 22 | 21 | 18 | $61

W Village | 50 Commerce St. (Barrow St.) | 212-524-2301

A "worthy renovation" of a "storied" West Village location (the former Grange Hall), this "sceney" New American offers "carefully conceived" dishes in "beautiful" surroundings adorned with a "WPA-style mural" and "deco bar"; the downsides are "service kinks" and "deafening" acoustics.

	FOOD	DECOR	SERVICE	COST
Keens Steakhouse *Steak*	24	23	22	$67

Garment District | 72 W. 36th St. (bet. 5th & 6th Aves.) | 212-947-3636 | www.keens.com

"Meat lovers" and history lovers praise this circa-1885 Garment District steakhouse/bar/party space where over 80,000 "clay pipes line the ceiling" and the signature "mutton chop is king"; "first-rate service", "Grover Cleveland"-worthy portions and a "treasure trove" of Americana add to the museum-quality appeal; in sum, well worth the splurge.

	FOOD	DECOR	SERVICE	COST
Pete's Tavern ◐ *Pub Food*	13	15	15	$31

Gramercy | 129 E. 18th St. (Irving Pl.) | 212-473-7676

"Rub elbows with history" over burgers and other "comforting" fare at Gramercy's "old-school haunt" where "O. Henry swilled, dined" and wrote "his knock 'em dead endings"; those who call the food "so-so" "grab a drink" at the bar - it's a "beautiful, nostalgic experience."

	FOOD	DECOR	SERVICE	COST
Russian Tea Room *Continental/Russian*	19	24	20	$72

W 50s | 150 W. 57th St. (bet. 6th & 7th Aves.) | 212-581-7100 | www.russiantearoomnyc.com

This "over-the-top" Russian-accented Continental Midtown "jewel box" is back and hailed by fans as "better than ever", though non-fans report "the life isn't there the way it once was" and say it's "for tourists alone"; all agree it's as "hard to kill as Rasputin" and costs plenty of rubles.

	FOOD	DECOR	SERVICE	COST
Waverly Inn and Garden ◐ *American*	19	21	18	$65

W Village | 16 Bank St. (Waverly Pl.) | 212-243-7900

Packing in more models than 7th on Sixth and "more celebs than the Oscars", complete with sidewalk "paparazzi", this charmingly restored 1920s West Village tavern owned by *Vanity Fair* editor Graydon Carter offers a "homestyle" menu with Hollywood touches; reservations can't be made by phone, but walk-ins are accepted - just go early or very late.

HOTEL DINING (ROOM OPTIONAL)

Work the segue upstairs, if things go well

	FOOD	DECOR	SERVICE	COST
Ago *Italian*	17	21	18	$79

TriBeCa | The Greenwich Hotel | 379 Greenwich St. (N. Moore St.) | 212-925-3797

Robert De Niro's latest TriBeCa endeavor is an "attractive" Tuscan spin-off of siblings in Hollywood, Vegas and South Beach; the food is "good", but not good enough to justify the "expensive" tabs and service still working out "early-days" kinks, though a bar scene for "young, fabulous" types helps.

Café Boulud *French* 27 | 23 | 26 | $84

E 70s | Surrey Hotel | 20 E. 76th St. (bet. 5th & Madison Aves.) | 212-772-2600 | www.danielnyc.com

"Comfortable" yet "civilized", Daniel Boulud's "sophisticated" Upper East Side satellite provides "glorious" dining thanks to chef Gavin Kaysen's "exquisite" French cuisine, "interesting" wines and "seamless service"; though decidedly "costly", prices are "less astronomical" than at the flagship, especially for the "bargain" $40 lunch prix fixe.

Gemma ◐ *Italian* 19 | 22 | 17 | $47

E Village | Bowery Hotel | 335 Bowery (bet. 2nd & 3rd Sts.) | 212-505-9100 | www.theboweryhotel.com

Parked on the burgeoning Bowery, this East Village Italian "hot spot" appeals to a "young crowd" that reports the food is "surprisingly good" though the rustic "atmosphere is better" (think "dark wood, copper pots, dripping candles"); service is "on cue" and prices are "decent", leaving the "no-reservations policy" as the only drawback to mention.

Kittichai *Thai* 22 | 27 | 20 | $60

SoHo | 60 Thompson Hotel | 60 Thompson St. (bet. Broome & Spring Sts.) | 212-219-2000 | www.kittichairestaurant.com

"Theatrical" decor (including a "pond with floating candles and orchids") nearly overwhelms the "innovative" food at this "so-hip-it-hurts" Thai where "stylish" sorts struggle to be heard over the "loud music"; sure, "it's pricey" and the "model-like" staff exudes "attitude", but let's face it, "it's SoHo."

Koi *Japanese* 24 | 23 | 18 | $65

W 40s | Bryant Park Hotel | 40 W. 40th St. (bet. 5th & 6th Aves.) | 212-921-3330 | www.koirestaurant.com

This "über-trendy" Midtown Japanese offers "creative" sushi and "delicious" fusion dishes in a "sleek", "sophisticated" setting; its "loud, youthful" crowd makes for "good people-watching", offsetting the "silly" prices and sometimes "indifferent" service.

La Bottega ◐ *Italian/Pizza* | 16 | 20 | 15 | $40

Chelsea | Maritime Hotel | 88 Ninth Ave. (17th St.) | 212-243-8400 | www.themaritimehotel.com

"If you can snag a table outside" on the "beautiful patio" when the "weather's fine", this "sceney" Chelsea Italian is "the place to be"; most are willing to "forgive" the "slow" service and "just-ok" food at "high prices" here given the "privilege of watching the trendy people" at play.

Olives *Mediterranean* | 22 | 21 | 20 | $58

Union Sq | W Union Sq. | 201 Park Ave. S. (17th St.) | 212-353-8345 | www.toddenglish.com

"Todd English doesn't disappoint" at this "upscale" Mediterranean in the W Union Square Hotel, where the "solid", "creative cuisine" is "well worth" the "expense-account" pricing; with a "jumping social scene" in the "bustling bar", "everything is pleasurable" except perhaps the "din."

MEET FOR A DRINK

For first dates, blind dates and other encounters with the unknown

Eleven Madison Park *French* | 27 | 26 | 26 | E

Gramercy | 11 Madison Ave. (24th St.) | 212-889-0905 | www.elevenmadisonpark.com

The "epitome of class", Danny Meyer's "magnificent" New French fronting Madison Square Park "wows the palate" with Daniel Humm's cuisine, following through with "sterling" service and a "stately", "soaring" art deco space; despite snipes at "elf"-size portions and "stratospherically priced" prix fixes, a clear majority is "happy to pay" for such "effortless indulgence."

Nobu 57 ◐ *Japanese* | 26 | 24 | 22 | VE

W 50s | 40 W. 57th St. (bet. 5th & 6th Aves.) | 212-757-3000 | www.noburestaurants.com

Entrée is more "accessible", but otherwise this Midtown "wow" "lives up to the name" of its Downtown forerunner as "bankers" and "beautiful people" "pack" David Rockwell's "cavernous", "high-style" space for "sensational" Japanese-Peruvian cuisine from an "informed" staff; the "celeb"-centric "hot scene" is "everything it's cracked up to be", but prepare to "leave your paycheck" behind.

Picholine *French/Mediterranean* 26 | 24 | 25 | VE

W 60s | 35 W. 64th St. (bet. B'way & CPW) | 212-724-8585 | www.picholinenyc.com

"Superb" prix fixe-only meals "elegantly served" in one of NYC's "most civilized rooms" is what diners find at Terry Brennan's "temple" to "fine" French-Mediterranean cuisine - and all "hail" the famously "divine" cheese cart; for a "memorable" evening, especially "followed by a short stroll to the Met", it's "as close to a sure thing as there is"; P.S. the new wine-and-fromage bar is a "wonderful" alternative.

Scarpetta *Italian* 26 | 24 | 23 | E

Chelsea | 355 W. 14th St. (bet. 8th & 9th Aves.) | 212-691-0555 | www.scarpettanyc.com

Chef Scott Conant (ex L'Impero) "hits a home run" with this new Chelsea Italian where his trademark "bright, flavorful" dishes are served by a "hospitable" staff; the dining room features a "wow"-worthy crowd and a "retractable" skylight, so "way-expensive" prices are the only rub.

Smith's *American* 22 | 21 | 22 | E

G Village | 79 MacDougal St. (bet. Bleecker & Houston Sts.) | 212-260-0100 | www.smithsnyc.com

Cindy Smith (Raoul's) and Danny Abrams (Red Cat) join forces with this "bright new" Villager, already a "winner" thanks to its "terrific" New American fare and "sunny" "pro" service; its narrow dining room evoking a "railway car" and "hip" back bar "transport you to the '40s."

Spice Market ◐ *SE Asian* 22 | 26 | 20 | VE

Meatpacking | 403 W. 13th St. (9th Ave.) | 212-675-2322 | www.jean-georges.com

From the "stunning" two-floor setting to the "sublime" Southeast Asian "street vendor" cuisine, Jean-Georges Vongerichten's Meatpacking District "fantasy" market is "a feast for the senses"; with "hot" staffers in "racy outfits" serving a "cool" "eye-candy" crowd, it's a "must-visit" - and those downstairs party rooms are a must-stay.

Union Square Cafe *American* 27 | 23 | 26 | E

Union Sq | 21 E. 16th St. (bet. 5th Ave. & Union Sq. W.) | 212-243-4020 | www.unionsquarecafe.com

Danny Meyer's Union Square "classic" is once again "top of the heap" - voted NYC's Most Popular - with new executive chef Carmen Quagliata overseeing the kitchen and its "beautifully composed" New American cuisine "honoring" "seasonal" ingredients; the experience of a "fundamentally perfect meal" is completed by the service ("top-tier but down-to-earth") and setting ("lovely" "without pretense"); N.B. if you can't score reservations, "go spur-of-the-moment" and dine at the "lively" bar.

MUSEUM VENUES

Dinner and a Monet

Café Sabarsky/Café Fledermaus *Austrian* 21 23 19 $42

E 80s | Neue Galerie | 1048 Fifth Ave. (86th St.) | 212-288-0665 | www.wallse.com

"Divine" desserts begging the question "art or tart?" are yours at Kurt Gutenbrunner's "charming" Austrian *kaffeehaus* in the UES Neue Galerie, where "fin de siècle Vienna comes alive" via a "sinful array" of "otherworldly" treats; as a result, "long queues" are common, though the "more casual" Fledermaus downstairs is usually less packed.

Modern, The 🅂 *American/French* 26 26 24 $111

W 50s | Museum of Modern Art | 9 W. 53rd St. (bet. 5th & 6th Aves.) | 212-333-1220 | www.themodernnyc.com

Chef Gabriel Kreuther's French-New American cuisine is so "inspired" it "could have been curated" at this MoMA "masterpiece" from Danny Meyer, where the "one-of-a-kind" "luxe setting" with a "splendid view" of the sculpture garden is overseen by a "superb" staff; while it's "well worth" the "platinum" pricing, the "stylish" but "less formal" bar's "exciting" small plates are "easier on the wallet."

Morgan, The 🄼 *American* 21 22 20 $45

Murray Hill | The Morgan Library & Museum | 225 Madison Ave. (bet. 36th & 37th Sts.) | 212-683-2130 | www.themorgan.org

"Dress like a blue blood" for lunch at Murray Hill's Morgan Library, either in the "pleasant" atrium cafe or the "classy" enclave "converted" from J. Pierpont's dining room; given the "well-executed" New American food, the "modern"-meets-"historic" atmosphere is sure to "grow on you."

Sarabeth's 🄼 *American* 20 17 17 $34

E 70s | Whitney Museum | 945 Madison Ave. (75th St.) | 212-570-3670 | www.sarabeth.com

This "cheerful" Whitney Museum spin-off of the American "lunching ladies" chainlet is an all-day-"breakfast mecca" and "tops for brunch" as well as offering lunch and dessert menus; "wobbly" service and "mile-long" "queues can be a pain", but it makes a good stop for a mid-gallery sit-down break.

NOTABLE OPENINGS

Because you know what's hot

Bar Blanc *French/Italian* 23 | 23 | 20 | $65

G Village | 142 W. 10th St. (bet. Greenwich Ave. & 7th Ave. S.) | 212-255-2330 | www.barblanc.com

A trio of Bouley alums are off to a "strong" start at this "chic" Village newcomer purveying "inventive", "skillfully prepared" French-Italian dishes; the "slinky", white-on-white space draws a "sophisticated" following that tolerates tabs that are "a little pricier than they need to be."

Bobo *European* 21 | 23 | 20 | $66

W Village | 181 W. 10th St. (7th Ave. S.) | 212-488-2626 | www.bobonyc.com

Set in a "beautiful brownstone", this soigné new Villager offers lots of "romantic" potential, with a moody subterranean bar, antiques-bedecked dining room and alfresco terrace; despite many "changes in the kitchen", the European fare is "delicious" and the "cool young" crowd doesn't seem to mind the upscale tabs.

Café Select *Swiss* - | - | - | M

SoHo | 212 Lafayette St. (bet. Broome & Spring Sts.) | 212-925-9322 | www.cafeselectnyc.com

Modern Swiss fare paired with Alpine wines arrives in SoHo at this reasonably priced new cafe serving breakfast, lunch and dinner; boho chic design - an artfully distressed paint job, posters stuck to the walls, a train station-size Rolex clock - reflects its nonchalant vibe, and since Downtown impresario Serge Becker (La Esquina) is involved, expect scenesters galore; N.B. they don't take reservations, so prime-time waits come with the territory.

Delicatessen ◐ *American* - | - | - | M

NoLita | 54 Prince St. (Lafayette St.) | 212-226-0211 | www.delicatessennyc.com

Spun off from the longtime Chelsea favorite Cafeteria, this NoLita newcomer boasts a similarly deadpan moniker along with the same slick modern looks, jazzed up American comfort-food eats and late-night hours; retractable streetside walls that open up in temperate weather make dropping in easy.

dell'anima ◐ *Italian* | 24 | 18 | 21 | $54

W Village | 38 Eighth Ave. (bet. Jane & W. 12th Sts.) | 212-366-6633 | www.dellanima.com

"Trendiness" has made this "intimate" West Village newcomer a "cheek-by-jowl" experience thanks to its "superlative" rustic Italian grub ("dell'icious pastas") and "impressive", "well-priced" vinos; it's "worth the effort" to score a table, and you can "see all the action" from the kitchen-side "chef's counter."

Double Crown *Eclectic* | - | - | - | E

NoHo | 316 Bowery St. (Bleecker St.) | 212-254-0350 | www.doublecrown-nyc.com

Opened by the ultrahip restaurant design firm AvroKO (which also owns Public), this NoHo stunner features characteristic exposed brick and industrial-vintage elements, including plenty of intricate carved-wood paneling; the ambitious Eclectic menu seeks to evoke the Indo-Asian corners of the former British Empire, but judging from the fabulous crowd and free-flowing cocktails, it's more about the scene here; N.B. there's also sidewalk seating and an adjacent lounge, Madam Geneva.

Elettaria ◐ *American* | ∇ 23 | 21 | 21 | $54

G Village | 33 W. Eighth St. (bet. 5th & 6th Aves.) | 212-677-3833 | www.elettarianyc.com

A "welcome change", this "trendy" Village newcomer with an "open kitchen" spices up its "terrific" New American lineup with a "hint of India"; the rustic room's "close seating" has everyone "rubbing elbows", but with "amazing mixology" and "sweet" service, surveyors sense a "hit."

Kingswood *Australian* | ∇ 21 | 20 | 18 | $49

G Village | 121 W. 10th St. (bet. Greenwich & 6th Aves.) | 212-645-0018 | www.kingswoodnyc.com

"Young", "too-cool-for-school" types are buzzing about this "trendy" new Village gastropub, serving "delicious" Australian-accented Americana; while both the room and crowd are "attractive", the "lively" "table-hopping" makes for "incredibly loud" dining.

Mia Dona *Italian* 21 | 18 | 19 | $53

E 50s | 206 E. 58th St. (bet. 2nd & 3rd Aves.) | 212-750-8170 | www.miadona.com

Michael Psilakis and Donatella Arpaia "have created another winner" with this "welcoming" East Side Italian featuring "rustic" yet "innovative" fare in "sleek" (some say "sterile") environs; though the staff perhaps is "still getting its footing", most agree that overall it's "off to a good start."

OPEN LATE FOR DINNER

For when you don't want the evening to end

Bar Milano ◐ *Italian* 22 | 22 | 21 | $61

Gramercy | 323 Third Ave. (24th St.) | 212-683-3035 | www.barmilano.com

The Denton brothers ('ino, 'inoteca, Lupa) bring Milan chic to Gramercy with this new, three-meals-a-day Northern Italian complete with a "happening" bar, "spot-on" menu, "excellent" wine list and "attentive" staff; despite its "ambitious" aspirations, the "high decibels" and "high prices" need some finessing.

Blue Ribbon ◐ *American* 24 | 18 | 22 | $51

SoHo | 97 Sullivan St. (bet. Prince & Spring Sts.) | 212-274-0404
Park Slope | 280 Fifth Ave. (bet. 1st St. & Garfield Pl.) | Brooklyn | 718-840-0404
www.blueribbonrestaurants.com

At these "always busy", "night owl"-friendly New Americans in SoHo and Park Slope, the Bromberg brothers purvey "eclectic", "ridiculously extensive" menus that "satisfy cravings" from "the simple to the sublime"; an "unfailingly friendly" staff sets a mood so "cheerful" that admirers overlook the "hefty waits" and "pricey" tabs for "gourmet dining, even at midnight."

Cafeteria ◐ *American* 18 | 15 | 14 | $32

Chelsea | 119 Seventh Ave. (17th St.) | 212-414-1717

The "people-watching may be more delicious than the food" at this "boisterous" Chelsea American where everyone from "brunch-seekers" to "club bunnies" pile in for midpriced comfort grub ferried by a staff with "heavy-duty attitude"; even though it's open "24 hours a day", some find it "a bit five minutes ago."

	FOOD	DECOR	SERVICE	COST
Empire Diner ◐ *Diner*	15	14	14	$25

Chelsea | 210 10th Ave. (22nd St.) | 212-243-2736

Like a "time machine", this "Chelsea fixture" slings "competent" diner grub 24/7 to everyone from "gallery-hoppers" to "clubbers" drawn to its 1929 "deco charm" and "great outside seating"; it's particularly "cool" at 3 AM, when its young, highly watchable crowd is especially oblivious to the prices and "aloof servers."

	FOOD	DECOR	SERVICE	COST
Employees Only ◐ *European*	19	20	19	$45

W Village | 510 Hudson St. (bet. Christopher & W. 10th Sts.) | 212-242-3021 | www.employeesonlynyc.com

"Young" types get "social" over "handcrafted cocktails" at this "lively" West Villager, a "fantastic little speakeasy" replica with a "charming" garden; while best "known for the drinks", it also serves "quite good" European fare into the wee hours, when some "wish it were half as full."

	FOOD	DECOR	SERVICE	COST
Frank ◐ *Italian*	23	14	16	$33

E Village | 88 Second Ave. (bet. 5th & 6th Sts.) | 212-420-0202 | www.frankrestaurant.com

"Size doesn't matter" at this ultra-"tiny", no-reservations East Villager offering "simply amazing" "homestyle" Italian food served in "scruffy", "bustling" quarters with "rock-concert" noise levels; considering that the cash-only costs are such a "steal", "long waits" are "inevitable."

	FOOD	DECOR	SERVICE	COST
La Esquina ◐ *Mexican*	22	20	17	$43

Little Italy | 106 Kenmare St. (bet. Cleveland Pl. & Lafayette St.) | 646-613-7100 | www.esquinanyc.com

A "secret-society attitude" and "snooty" bouncer set the tone for the "speakeasy-style" brasserie/tequila bar downstairs at this Little Italy Mexican; to "avoid the scene", try the "amazing" take-out taqueria for "*guapos*" tacos or the "chilled-out" cafe for "tasty", "simple" fare.

	FOOD	DECOR	SERVICE	COST
Momofuku Ssäm Bar ◐ *American*	23	15	17	$41

E Village | 207 Second Ave. (13th St.) | 212-254-3500 | www.momofuku.com

Admiring multitudes "can't get enough" of David Chang's "brilliant" "flavor combos" at this roomier East Village adjunct of his Noodle Bar, an "informal" destination for "luscious" Asian-influenced New American creations; whether for burrito-esque *ssäms* at lunch or a "more sophisticated" dinner, the "bench seating" "fills up fast", so "be prepared to wait"; N.B. a renovation is in the works that will add a pastry kitchen.

Spotted Pig ◐ *Gastropub* 22 | 18 | 16 | $46

W Village | 314 W. 11th St. (Greenwich St.) | 212-620-0393 | www.thespottedpig.com

"Pretty people", "celebs" and many of NYC's "top" toques "clamor to get in" to this "witty" Village gastropub for April Bloomfield's "spot-on" Modern European eats; it's "all the rage", so "hurried service" and "killer waits" are a "given", unless you "go at off hours" (fortunately, the kitchen's open till 2 AM).

RAW BARS

Even if the aphrodisiac qualities are all in your head

Aquagrill *Seafood* 26 | 19 | 23 | $58

SoHo | 210 Spring St. (6th Ave.) | 212-274-0505 | www.aquagrill.com

"Seafood right off the boat" prepared by chef Jeremy Marshall plus "oysters galore" from a "knockout raw bar" are served by "spot-on" staffers at this "love-at-first-bite" SoHo piscatorium where's it's "fun to sit at the bar and watch the shuckers"; "crowbar" seating and "high prices" aside, it's only "getting better with age."

bar Q *Pan-Asian* ▽ 20 | 18 | 21 | $53

W Village | 308-310 Bleecker St. (bet. Grove St. & 7th Ave. S.) | 212-206-7817 | www.barqrestaurant.com

Anita Lo's "distinctive" cooking has a new West Village showcase at this "casual" Asian barbecue-cum-raw bar set in "minimalist", "stark white" digs with a greenhouse atrium; overall, this enterprise is "almost there."

Blue Fin ◐ *Seafood* 21 | 22 | 19 | $56

W 40s | W Times Sq. | 1567 Broadway (47th St.) | 212-918-1400 | www.brguestrestaurants.com

Bringing "destination" dining to Times Square, Steve Hanson's "popular" seafooder vends "swimmingly fresh" fish in its "lively" street-level cafe as well as a "more relaxed" upstairs room; despite "high decibels" and "uneven service", fans are willing to "pay the premium" for the "primo location" alone.

City Hall ☒ *Seafood/Steak* 20 | 21 | 20 | $57

TriBeCa | 131 Duane St. (bet. Church St. & W. B'way) | 212-227-7777 | www.cityhallnyc.com

The "red-suspender set" - think "local pols" and other city "bigwigs" - wheel and deal at this "standout" TriBeCa surf 'n' turfer from Henry Meer, where "terrific", "top-dollar" grub is served in "spiffy digs" (or in "great party rooms" downstairs); the mood is "historic" and "fast-moving", kinda "like NYC" itself.

Mermaid Inn *Seafood* 21 | 17 | 19 | $46

E Village | 96 Second Ave. (bet. 5th & 6th Sts.) | 212-674-5870
W 80s | 568 Amsterdam Ave. (bet. 87th & 88th Sts.) | 212-799-7400
www.themermaidnyc.com

This "perennial" East Village "favorite" for "solid", "dependable" seafood has taken its "fish shack" formula uptown (finally, "killer" "lobster rolls on the UWS!"); both locations are often "crowded" and "noisy", so, "small seaside town feel" notwithstanding, repasts here are often more "festive" than relaxing.

Oyster Bar ☒ *Seafood* 21 | 17 | 16 | $48

E 40s | Grand Central | lower level (42nd St. & Vanderbilt Ave.) | 212-490-6650 | www.oysterbarny.com

Traditionalists "treasure" this "time-honored" Grand Central seafood "standard-bearer" for its "amazing assortment" of "impeccable oysters", "classic" pan roasts and "perfectly prepared" fish, paired with "the best" white wines; its "massive" tiled arches may at times echo with the "overwhelming" "din", but it's "hard to top" as a Gotham "must-visit."

ROMANTIC CELEBRATING

From one-month anniversary to marriage proposal, where to do it right

Allen & Delancey ◐ *American* 24 | 24 | 20 | $67

LES | 115 Allen St. (Delancey St.) | 212-253-5400 | www.allenanddelancey.net

"Luxury dining" comes to the LES via this "edgy" yet "polished" New American turning out "marvelous" "high-end" meals in a "divine", brick-walled setting "lit with many candles"; "amiable service" enhances a mood so "seductive" that romeos report "if you can't seal the deal here, you may as well quit"; N.B. the departure of chef Neil Ferguson puts its Food score in question.

	FOOD	DECOR	SERVICE	COST

Mas *American* 28 | 24 | 26 | $75

G Village | 39 Downing St. (bet. Bedford & Varick Sts.) | 212-255-1790 | www.masfarmhouse.com

"Close to dining perfection", this "elegant yet hip" New American Villager is an oasis of "casual" refinement where the "wonderful, market-fresh" cooking by Galen Zamarra is delivered by a "warm" crew in quarters that are "romantic" but nonetheless "not too quiet"; all this "pricey" sophistication means it's "like no *mas*" (farmhouse) most have ever encountered.

One if by Land, Two if by Sea *American* 24 | 27 | 24 | $101

G Village | 17 Barrow St. (bet. 7th Ave. S. & W. 4th St.) | 212-228-0822 | www.oneifbyland.com

"Bring the ring" and "hope she says yes" is the theme at this Village New American, which transforms "Aaron Burr's" circa-1767 carriage house into a "romantic landmark"; after the "remarkable" $75 prix fixe menu, "cosseting" service and "classy" backdrop featuring "candlelight" and a pianist, she's bound to accept any proposal; since "they've renovated and brought in a new chef", the "wallet stress" is even more justified.

Raoul's ● *French* 23 | 20 | 20 | $55

SoHo | 180 Prince St. (bet. Sullivan & Thompson Sts.) | 212-966-3518 | www.raouls.com

A "SoHo standby" since 1975, this "sexy" French "classic" with a dark "backstreet Paris" air sets the "gold standard" for "hip, authentic" New York City bistros; never mind if it's "a little expensive", thanks to "incredible" cooking and that "dream" of a "hideaway garden", it's "still hot."

River Café *American* 26 | 27 | 25 | $127

Dumbo | 1 Water St. (bet. Furman & Old Fulton Sts.) | Brooklyn | 718-522-5200 | www.rivercafe.com

"Million dollar views" of Manhattan and the East River, "sublime" New American cuisine, "dignified, relaxed service" and a "flower-filled" room make a "sybaritic brew" - aka Dumbo's "grand luxe" "treat"; "it's under the Brooklyn Bridge but over the moon", with tabs to match ($98 prix fixe-only dinners), though all agree that it's a "magical" experience "well worth the splurge"; N.B. jackets required.

	FOOD	DECOR	SERVICE	COST
Suba ◐ *Spanish*	20	24	20	$54

LES | 109 Ludlow St. (bet. Delancey & Rivington Sts.) | 212-982-5714 | www.subanyc.com

"Dramatic" decor featuring "flowing water" in a "romantic grotto" room is the highlight at this "hip" LES Spaniard, however its "upscale riffs on classic" Iberian cuisine are also draws; add "helpful" service and a "sexy bar scene" and it's "perfect for dates."

TASTING MENUS

When you know you want to spend four hours together

	FOOD	DECOR	SERVICE	COST
Adour *French*	26	27	26	$120

E 50s | St. Regis Hotel | 2 E. 55th St. (bet. 5th & Madison Aves.) | 212-710-2277 | www.adour-stregis.com

A "triumph for Monsieur Ducasse", this "glamorous" new Midtown French in the St. Regis offers "sophisticated", "wine-centric" dining in a "sumptuous" David Rockwell makeover of the former Lespinasse space; chef Tony Esnault's "approachable" yet *très*-haute menu is "sublime on all counts" and service is equally "flawless", so even though it "wallops the wallet", most agree it's nothing less than "wonderful."

	FOOD	DECOR	SERVICE	COST
Cru ⊠ *European*	26	23	25	$109

G Village | 24 Fifth Ave. (bet. 9th & 10th Sts.) | 212-529-1700 | www.cru-nyc.com

A "cast-of-thousands" wine list draws "vinophiles" to this "outstanding" Villager, backed up by "sublime" Modern European cooking, "impeccable" service and a "pleasant" if "sterile" setting; prix fixe-only menus ($84 and up) make for "blow-the-kids'-college-fund" dining, but cheaper à la carte options are available in the walk-ins-only front room.

	FOOD	DECOR	SERVICE	COST
Del Posto *Italian*	26	27	25	$91

Chelsea | 85 10th Ave. (16th St.) | 212-497-8090 | www.delposto.com

A "large-scale" "sensory experience" from the Batali-Bastianich team, this Way West Chelsea "haute Italian" "wows" with "delectable" cuisine and an "off-the-charts" wine list presented in a "lavish", marble-and-mahogany room recalling a "majestic palazzo"; "exceptional service" rounds out the "tour de force" dining experience, and though "sticker shock" is likely, the "enoteca is a total bargain."

EN Japanese Brasserie *Japanese* 23 | 25 | 21 | $57

W Village | 435 Hudson St. (Leroy St.) | 212-647-9196 | www.enjb.com

En-thusiasts en-dorse this "spacious" West Village "eye-opener" for its "swank"-meets-"Zen" ambiance and equally "impressive" menu of "different" Japanese small plates (many showcasing "superb fresh tofu"); an "endless sake list" and "lovely" service encourage "tranquility" - at least until you see the tab.

Jewel Bako ◐ ⊠ *Japanese* 25 | 22 | 23 | $80

E Village | 239 E. Fifth St. (bet. 2nd & 3rd Aves.) | 212-979-1012

"Hidden away" in a "tiny" East Village storefront, this chic Japanese enjoys a "well-deserved reputation" for "sexy sushi" served in "fashionable", bamboo-lined digs; the "terrific service" is overseen by "hosts-with-the-most" Jack and Grace Lamb, and the overall mood is "serene - until the check arrives."

L'Atelier de Joël Robuchon *French* 28 | 25 | 26 | $127

E 50s | Four Seasons Hotel | 57 E. 57th St. (bet. Madison & Park Aves.) | 212-350-6658 | www.fourseasons.com

"Exquisite in every way", "genius" chef Joël Robuchon's "stunning" Japanese-influenced Midtown French outpost offers "sublime", "almost-too-beautiful-to-eat" small plates that achieve "absolute purity of flavor"; sit at the "sushi bar"-style counter and "watch the chefs at work" while being attended to by a "pleasant" pro staff - but "be prepared to mortgage your apartment" because "perfection doesn't come cheap."

Momofuku Ko *American* 26 | 18 | 22 | $130

E Village | 163 First Ave. (bet. 10th & 11th Sts.) | 212-475-7899 | www.momofuku.com

"David Chang has done it again" at this gustatory "high temple" in a minimalist East Village space, where the "lucky" ko-hort at the "12-seater" tasting bar watches "cutting-edge" chefs prepare "flawless", "adventurous" prix fixe-only Asian-accented New American fare; it's "euphoria" provided you can crack the "radical egalitarian" web-only reservation system and are "prepared to spend" (the price is market-based, but ranges from $85-110); N.B. it recently started serving lunch Friday-Sunday, with a menu more elaborate and expensive than dinner.

Nightlife

	APPEAL	DECOR	SERVICE	COST

ART BARS

Cocktails + culture

Box, The

APPEAL	DECOR	SERVICE	COST
25	23	19	$18

LES | 189 Chrystie St. (bet. Rivington & Stanton Sts.) | 212-982-9301 | www.theboxnyc.com

"Expect the wild and the unexpected" at this "steamy", late-night LES supper club, a "Victorianish" cabaret where "naughty" performers engage in "vaudeville" acts, "over-the-top burlesque" and overall "debauchery" suggesting the "decline of Western civilization"; be prepared to "throw money to the wind", and since it's one of the "hottest" scenes around, "good luck getting in."

Half King

APPEAL	DECOR	SERVICE	COST
19	15	19	$8

Chelsea | 505 W. 23rd St. (10th Ave.) | 212-462-4300 | www.thehalfking.com

A "low-key alternative to the hipper-than-hip" alternatives in West Chelsea, this "simple" Irish pub-cum-"literati" salon draws "interesting" folk with its weekly "book readings", rotating "photography" exhibits and "late-night hipster cruising" opportunities; it's spread out over "lots of different rooms", but that "nice backyard" garden is the real crowd-pleaser.

KGB Bar

APPEAL	DECOR	SERVICE	COST
21	17	18	$7

E Village | 85 E. Fourth St., 2nd fl. (bet. 2nd & 3rd Aves.) | 212-505-3360 | www.kgbbar.com

"Drinks and readings" coexist peacefully at this "small" East Village theme bar with an "off-the-grid", "cool Kremlin" vibe (it looks like a "living room" crossed with a "Soviet-era Moscow pub"); accessed by a "narrow stairwell", it lures a "strange but fun" mix of "intelligentsia" types and showcases the work of "lots of writers" and poets.

Monkey Town

APPEAL	DECOR	SERVICE	COST
▽ 21	24	21	$8

Williamsburg | 58 N. Third St. (bet. Kent & Wythe Aves.) | Brooklyn | 718-384-1369 | www.monkeytownhq.com

Video art is the name of the game at this "novel" Williamsburg eatery/performance space where the festively decorated front dining room is overshadowed by a spectacular back area fitted out on all four walls with mammoth screens; the programming ranges from the "indie" to the mainstream, though its "bathroom soundscapes" are pointedly avant-garde.

Nublu ⇏ 26 | 18 | 18 | $10

E Village | 62 Ave. C (bet. 4th & 5th Sts.) | www.nublu.net
"Diverse" crowds keep things interesting at this "spunky", "offbeat" Alphabet City lounge, a midsize spot with "quirky", bachelor-pad looks and a "nice back patio"; "lively" musicians and "talented" DJs play everything from "funk and hip-hop to dance and world music", but no matter what's on the agenda, it usually "feels real" here.

Supreme Trading 23 | 21 | 20 | $9

Williamsburg | 213 N. Eighth St. (bet. Driggs Ave. & Roebling St.) | Brooklyn | 718-599-4224 | www.supremetradingny.com
Packing "lots of different environments" into one sprawling space, this "cool" Williamsburger offers bar, lounge and art exhibition options topped off by an "outside smoking patio"; sure, it's usually "filled with hipsters", but a "general sense of goodwill" pervades - "no one's too cool for school here."

BOTTLE SERVICE

When the night is worth a splurge

Cain Luxe 24 | 24 | 19 | $16

Chelsea | 544 W. 27th St. (bet. 10th & 11th Aves.) | 212-947-8000 | www.cainnyc.com
"A-listers" shake their booties to a "jungle beat" at this newly renovated West Chelsea "club phenomenon" that resembles a "wild African" game lodge and is frequented by tribes of "celebs", "rain-thin models" and "well-dressed bankers" blowing their cash on "exorbitant bottles"; anyone intent on happy "hunting" will have to "get past the impossible door" - "exclusivity is what it's all about."

Kiss & Fly 20 | 21 | 17 | $16

Meatpacking | 409 W. 13th St. (bet. 9th Ave. & Washington St.) | 212-255-1933 | www.kissandflyclub.com
"Beautiful people" breathe easy at this "hot" new Meatpacking District club (fka Aer) that brings on "techno" beats, "strobe lights" and "high rollers" partying under "Roman Coliseum" arches and "Michelangelo-

inspired" ceiling art; critics kiss it off as a "Eurotrash stomping ground", but many see "potential" behind the "expectedly tough door."

Marquee

23 | 22 | 17 | $15

Chelsea | 289 10th Ave. (bet. 26th & 27th Sts.) | 646-473-0202 | www.marqueeny.com

Sure, it's "been around awhile" and may be "a little more democratic" than before, but most report this West Chelsea club still provides the expected "door drama" unless you are "knockout gorgeous", "know somebody or, better yet, *are* somebody"; no surprise, it's "best during the week", the "most fun is in the VIP room" and, as for the service, "models might look good but they suck at waitressing."

1 Oak

22 | 20 | 18 | $16

Chelsea | 453 W. 17th St. (bet. 9th & 10th Aves.) | 212-242-1111 | www.1oaknyc.com

"Models, celebs and social climbers" are stoked for the "more intimate" lounging of yesteryear at this "much-hyped" new West Chelsea club that justifies its name ("stands for 'one of a kind'") with "fancy" quarters, "high energy" and "precision exclusion"; it's a "great night on the town" - provided you're ready to deal with one of the "hardest doors in NYC."

Pink Elephant

24 | 22 | 20 | $15

Chelsea | 527 W. 27th St. (bet. 10th & 11th Aves.) | 212-463-0000 | www.pinkelephantclub.com

"Well-hidden" underground on Chelsea's Bottle Service Row, this "exclusive" nightclub cranks up the smoke and "scent machines" for the amusement of its "attractive international" following; brace yourself for lots of "rich guys and anorexic girls", an "impossible" door manned by "uppity" bouncers and ultrahigh pricing.

Tenjune

25 | 21 | 19 | $15

Meatpacking | 26 Little W. 12th St., downstairs (bet. 9th Ave. & Washington St.) | 646-624-2410 | www.tenjunenyc.com

A "tough door" policy and "no elbow room" collide at this subterranean Meatpacking club that's "totally hot" for the moment - "until the next one comes along"; brace yourself for an "ultratrendy" crowd where "everyone looks like a model" (or an "overly groomed gold digger"), all "dancing their butts off", "bumping into the who's who" of the nightlife world and wishing they could "afford bottle service."

BOWLING & BOARD GAMES

Give yourselves something to focus on other than each other

Abilene
20 | 15 | 19 | $7

Carroll Gardens | 442 Court St. (3rd Pl.) | Brooklyn | 718-522-6900 | www.abilenebarbrooklyn.com

This "neighborhoody" Carroll Gardens watering hole is a "go-to" for "chilled-out locals" and a "great place to get to know the zillions of new people moving into the area"; amenities include "ice-breaking board games", "consistent Brooklyn people-watching" and "good tunes."

Bowlmor Lanes
22 | 17 | 14 | $11

G Village | 110 University Pl., 3rd fl. (bet. 12th & 13th Sts.) | 212-255-8188 | www.bowlmor.com

If that "jones to bowl" strikes, this "retro" Village alley is pimped out with "nightclublike" lights and music plus a full bar where "ultracool" players circulate; the booze, "per-frame" fee and "shoe rental" can get "pricey", but these are the "liveliest" lanes around, and when you're ready to roll "there aren't too many others" to pin hopes on.

Buttermilk Bar
23 | 15 | 20 | $7

Park Slope | 577 Fifth Ave. (16th St.) | Brooklyn | 718-788-6297

According to the "cool crowd" currently "gentrifying" South Park Slope, this "dark" bar "churns out great drinks" for low dough and throws in "hipster perks" like "old board games", pinball and an "excellent jukebox"; add occasional live "country music" and there's more than enough "good stuff" to "keep you entertained."

Dram Shop
- | - | - | M

Park Slope | 339 Ninth St. (bet. 5th & 6th Aves.) | Brooklyn | 718-788-1444

From the minds behind Angry Wade's, this new Park Sloper comes equipped with a long wooden bar, huge booths and a back patio; there's plenty of entertainment on hand - shuffleboard, pool, board games - all made merrier by an ample selection of tap brew, whiskey and bourbon.

Gutter, The
∇ 24 | 20 | 18 | $9

Greenpoint | 200 N. 14th St. (Berry St.) | Brooklyn | 718-387-3585 | www.thegutterbrooklyn.com

A "bar-and-bowling-alley" combination, this new Greenpoint joint combines eight "old-school" lanes with an equally "retro" taproom vending "cheap, well-selected" brews; it's "aptly named", what with the downscale atmosphere, but low rollers swear a "great time is had by all."

Kettle of Fish 21 | 16 | 20 | $8

G Village | 59 Christopher St. (bet. 7th Ave. S. & Waverly Pl.) | 212-414-2278 | www.kettleoffishnyc.com

There's "lots of room for lounging" at this "friendly" Village watering hole, plus "darts or board games" if you want to keep busy; it's "*the* place to be on Sunday night if you love the Packers" (the owners hail from Wisconsin), and even though there's "no kitchen", you can always "have food delivered."

Levee, The 19 | 17 | 21 | $7

Williamsburg | 212 Berry St. (N. 3rd St.) | Brooklyn | 718-218-8787 | www.theleveenyc.com

Run by "friendly" Texans, this funky Williamsburg watering hole is a "non-hipster hang in the heart of hipster heaven" where everything from "interesting" microbrews to "beer and whiskey combos" comes at "great prices"; "board games galore" and trashy snacks like "Frito pies" are bonuses.

Perdition 20 | 18 | 22 | $8

W 40s | 692 10th Ave. (bet. 48th & 49th Sts.) | 212-582-5660 | www.perditionnyc.com

An "out-of-the-way" location in Hell's Kitchen doesn't deter neighborhood locals from this "laid-back" Irish "hideaway" known for its "frequent drink specials" and board game library; a "welcoming" staff, "hands-on owners" and "plenty of room to stretch out" make it a "solid" destination.

300 New York 19 | 15 | 15 | $11

(fka Chelsea Piers Bowling Alley)

Chelsea | Chelsea Piers | Pier 60 (Hudson River & W. 18th St.) | 212-835-2695 | www.3hundred.com

Keglers who spend their spare time at this "pricey" Chelsea Piers lane/lounge combo report "good clean fun" via "awesome disco bowling" ("current music", "nice glow-in-the-dark effects") that evokes "middle school, but with vodka"; there's a bonus too: "no waits" on weeknights due to its way-West locale.

BOYS' NIGHT OUT

TVs and beer - no pretense

Blondies

19 | 13 | 20 | $8

E 90s | 1770 Second Ave. (bet. 92nd & 93rd Sts.) | 212-410-3300
W 70s | 212 W. 79th St. (bet. Amsterdam Ave. & B'way) | 212-362-4360
www.blondiessports.com

"Game-day nirvanas", these "pure sports bars" don't disappoint "avid" fans who turn up for the "cold brew priced right", "killer" Buffalo wings and, of course, "more TVs than customers"; so round up your "college buds" for some "yelling" and "fight songs", but go before the "big game" kicks off or else "it'll be impossible to find room."

Croxley Ales

20 | 16 | 16 | $7

E Village | 28 Ave. B (bet. 2nd & 3rd Sts.) | 212-253-6140 | www.croxley.com

Once a filling station, this "easygoing" indoor/outdoor sports bar in the East Village remains stereotypically male, featuring an "impressive international menu" of more than 100 beers, "cheap wings" and plenty of "big-screen TVs" ("you'll have no problem finding your game"); "slow" service is the main gripe.

40/40

21 | 21 | 17 | $15

Chelsea | 6 W. 25th St. (bet. B'way & 6th Ave.) | 212-832-4040 | www.the4040club.com

"If you've got game", "wear the right gear" and spectate "in style" at this Chelsea "hip-hop sports bar", a "swank", "spacious" testament to the "platinum" taste of co-owner Jay-Z (i.e. a gazillion flat-screens, "swinging lounge chairs" and a "cigar haunt upstairs"); prices are "sky high", but it's "crazy packed" with "bling"-bedecked playas anyway 'cause Hova "knows what works."

Jimmy's Corner

25 | 16 | 23 | $6

W 40s | 140 W. 44th St. (bet. B'way & 6th Ave.) | 212-221-9510

"So close, yet so far away from the Times Square hoopla", this "authentic dive" is a "tribute to boxing" festooned with pugilist "memorabilia" and owned by former prizefighter Jimmy Glenn; oozing "retro cool", it's a "long way from the sterile chain joints" in the area and "still good, even after the smoking ban."

	APPEAL	DECOR	SERVICE	COST
Tonic	19	20	18	$9

W 40s | 727 Seventh Ave. (bet. 48th & 49th Sts.) | 212-382-1059 | www.tonicbarnyc.com

The flat-screens are "gigantic" and the range of sporting events broadcast is "vast" at this "awesome" Times Square sports bar triplex that also "appeals to women" with its slick, shiny looks; sure, it's "touristy", given the location, but it's "good during happy hour" if you'd like to meet someone from Morgan Stanley, whose world headquarters is nearby.

COFFEEHOUSES

When you're going for casual and conversation-friendly

Arlo & Esme — - | - | - | M

E Village | 42 E. First St. (bet. 1st & 2nd Aves.) | 212-777-5617

A coffee shop grafted onto a bar/lounge, this new, something-for-everyone East Villager (set in the former Chez Es Saada digs) offers premium java and free WiFi in a squeaky clean upstairs room; after dark, the funkier, grotto-esque basement pours specialty cocktails, with Ms. Pac-Man and a pool table thrown in for good measure.

Cafe Gitane ⊄ — 22 | 18 | 15 | $9

NoLita | 242 Mott St. (bet. Houston & Prince Sts.) | 212-334-9552

"See and be seen" with a "cosmopolitan" crew at this "stylish" NoLita cafe that's perpetually "filled to the gills" with "Eurotrash" and "trust fund kids" ("don't these people have jobs?"); it's "so pretentious" that you can't help but "love it", but also so "small" that you can count on a "wait every time."

Caffe Reggio ⊄ — 20 | 18 | 16 | $9

G Village | 119 MacDougal St. (bet. Bleecker & W. 3rd Sts.) | 212-475-9557 | www.caffereggio.com

It's all about the "history" at this "quaint", '20s-era "Village staple", an "old-style Italian cafe" where the "antique furniture" and paintings make for a "cozy" backdrop for a "cappuccino-and-pastry" break; no alcohol is served, so primo "people-watching" provides the buzz.

Edgar's Cafe ⊄ — 21 | 17 | 17 | $10

W 80s | 255 W. 84th St. (bet. B'way & West End Ave.) | 212-496-6126

"Beat the crowds at Cafe Lalo" by opting for this UWS competitor, a "civilized" and slightly "more romantic" place to "meet and talk" late-night over "delicious desserts" and a glass of wine; service can be "rushed", but interiors designed to honor its namesake Edgar Allan Poe keep loyal literature lovers ravin'.

Grey Dog's Coffee
22 | 18 | 19 | $8

G Village | 33 Carmine St. (bet. Bedford & Bleecker Sts.) | 212-462-0041
G Village | 90 University Pl. (bet. 11th & 12th Sts.) | 212-414-4739
www.thegreydog.com

"Sort of like Central Perk but with alcohol" (i.e. beer and wine), this "quintessential" Village cafe is a "nice evening hangout" for "locals", "NYU" types and "golden retriever owners"; given the "relaxed atmosphere", it works with "friends, as well as with a date"; N.B. the new University Place outpost opened post-Survey.

Mocca
▽ 21 | 20 | 21 | $11

TriBeCa | 78 Reade St. (Church St.) | 212-233-7570 | www.moccalounge.com

Coffeehouse by day, lounge by night, this "small" but "upscale" TriBeCan is just the ticket when you "can't quite decide what you want"; large windows and a "pleasant" contemporary look make it a natural for after-work drinks spiced up by "good people-watching."

COMEDY CLUBS

Because what's more key than compatible humor?

Carolines
21 | 16 | 17 | $13

W 40s | 1626 Broadway (bet. 49th & 50th Sts.) | 212-757-4100 | www.carolines.com

Something "really funny" is going on at this renowned Times Square comedy club, a "top-notch" mecca of mirth where everyone from "great names" to "worthy new" wits works the room; if the "expensive" covers and "two-drink minimum" aren't as "laughable", it's still "worth it" to catch "some of the best" talent in the biz.

Comedy Cellar
23 | 13 | 16 | $10

G Village | 117 MacDougal St. (bet. Bleecker & W. 3rd Sts.) | 212-254-3480 | www.comedycellar.com

"Always a pick-me-upper", this subterranean Village grin bin has chuckleheads claiming it's got the "best ratio of hysterical-to-bombing comedians" around; a few kvetch about "closer-than-need-be quarters" and that two-drink minimum, but "surprise celebrity" visits by Chris Rock and other SNL alums turn most frowns upside down.

	APPEAL	DECOR	SERVICE	COST
Comix	∇ 23	21	21	$10

Chelsea | 353 W. 14th St. (bet. 8th & 9th Aves.) | 212-524-2500 | www.comixny.com

Fans are "psyched" about this "chichi" Chelsea venue, a 5,000-sq.-ft. spot that "offers much more" than comedy (i.e. "surprisingly" high-end New American eats), plus half-off happy hours and ambitious programming like the *American Idol*-esque stand-up competition; a few purists are dubious, saying "an 'upscale' comedy club is just not funny", but boosters say "ya gotta believe."

	APPEAL	DECOR	SERVICE	COST
Gotham Comedy Club	19	13	16	$13

Chelsea | 208 W. 23rd St. (bet. 7th & 8th Aves.) | 212-367-9000 | www.gothamcomedyclub.com

Now that's it's moved to a "cavernous", 10,000-sq.-ft. setting, this Chelsea comedy club has retained its "solid" talent, though some say the digs are "a bit too clean" and "commercial" for the genre; be aware that costs still "add up quickly" thanks to that "ridiculously pricey" two-drink minimum.

	APPEAL	DECOR	SERVICE	COST
Stand-Up NY Comedy Club	18	10	16	$14

W 70s | 236 W. 78th St. (bet. Amsterdam Ave. & B'way) | 212-595-0850 | www.standupny.com

"Pretty good" laughs lie ahead at this Upper West Side "neighborhood" comedy club where the "overpriced" drinks and "cramped" seating aren't so funny; overall, it's "decent but nothing spectacular", except for nights when brand-name comics (like Chris Rock and Robin Williams) drop by.

DANCE CLUBS

High-energy destinations for couples or groups

	APPEAL	DECOR	SERVICE	COST
Cielo	23	21	18	$14

Meatpacking | 18 Little W. 12th St. (bet. 9th Ave. & Washington St.) | 212-645-5700 | www.cieloclub.com

With a "futuristic" setting that includes a sunken blue "dancing pit", this "intimate" Meatpacking disco brings in "awesome international DJs" whose "Euro trance and house music" creates "transcendence despite the crush of bodies"; if the "eclectic" crowd is perhaps "less chic than it used to be", don't blame "pompous" bouncers who enforce a stringent "velvet-rope policy."

Pacha

20 | 20 | 16 | $13

W 40s | 618 W. 46th St. (bet. 11th & 12th Aves.) | 212-209-7500 | www.pachanyc.com

"Straight from Ibiza" comes this "fly" clubzilla, an outpost of the international dance club chain that naturally draws the "old Sound Factory crowd" since it occupies the same "infamous" Hell's Kitchen building; expect a "cavernous", four-story setup with "plenty of dark corners", big-name DJs and "half-naked" go-go gals showering inside glassed-in stalls; downsides include "rude service" and "long waits at the coat check."

Santos Party House

- | - | - | M

Chinatown | 100 Lafayette St. (bet. Walker & White Sts.) | 212-714-4646 | www.santospartyhouse.com

Good old-fashioned dancing till 4 AM comes to Chinatown via this new double-decker dance club-cum-music venue consisting of a black-walled, disco-balled ground floor with a more bare-bones basement below; look for a state-of-the-art sound system, turntables turned by hot-shot DJs and crowds of people trying to get in.

S.O.B.'s

22 | 16 | 17 | $12

SoHo | 204 Varick St. (Houston St.) | 212-243-4940 | www.sobs.com

If you're "serious about dancing the night away" to "eclectic world music" ("bhangra, reggae, salsa - the list is endless"), this 25-year-old SoHo Latin club is "still tons of fun" and as much of a "total party" as ever; you can always count on it for "high energy", though there are "different crowds, depending on the night" at this "something-for-everyone" spot.

Studio B

∇ 24 | 15 | 16 | $10

Greenpoint | 259 Banker St. (bet. Calyer St. & Meserole Ave.) | Brooklyn | 718-389-1880 | www.clubstudiob.com

"Escape Manhattan" at this "best-kept secret" in Greenpoint, a "cavernous" club-cum-concert space featuring a "worthy" slate of indie-darling bands, "bangin'" DJs and an expansive dance floor; getting there may be "a chore", but the "upbeat" attitude is bound to "please."

Touch

25 | 25 | 19 | $15

W 50s | 240 W. 52nd St. (bet. B'way & 8th Ave.) | 212-489-7656 | www.touchnewyorkcity.com

The "most Downtown spot" in Midtown is the early word on this "exciting" new megaclub, a "breath of fresh air" in a dead zone featuring an "amazing multilevel space" endowed with cushy perches, a "huge dance floor" and a futuristic, glows-on-contact bar; folks "tired of the Meatpacking District" scene say this one's "untouchable."

DRINK SPECIALISTS

Plan a theme night around your favorite cocktail

Brandy Library

25 | 26 | 24 | $14

TriBeCa | 25 N. Moore St. (bet. Hudson & Varick Sts.) | 212-226-5545 | www.brandylibrary.com

Check out the "perfect dram" at this "top-shelf" TriBeCa "temple of libation" that keeps "serious drinkers" in "fine spirits" with its "jaw-dropping selection"; channeling a "wood-paneled gentleman's club" with "bookshelves" stocked with bottles and "sophisticated" sommeliers, it appeals to "older" finance types who don't flinch at the "eye-popping tabs."

Bubble Lounge

22 | 20 | 19 | $14

TriBeCa | 228 W. Broadway (bet. Franklin & White Sts.) | 212-431-3433 | www.bubblelounge.com

"Wall Streeters" and "couples" out for a "sophisticated tryst" surface at this "plush" TriBeCa champagne lounge, a "sexy", "long-on-style" enclave of "faded opulence" that still delivers some "fizz"; but the "high-maintenance" tabs are "annoying" unless "your rich uncle is paying", and the trendsetters popped out "15 minutes ago."

d.b.a.

22 | 15 | 18 | $8

E Village | 41 First Ave. (bet. 2nd & 3rd Sts.) | 212-475-5097 | www.drinkgoodstuff.com

The name "should stand for 'Darn Best Ales'" declare devotees of this "always packed" East Village "beer-and-scotch drinkers' utopia" where the "intelligently chosen", rotating inventory is augmented by semi-regular tastings; the weatherproofed back garden remains "ideal" for "afternoon conversation", but cynics nix the "pretentious" service and "frightening" restrooms.

Death & Co

25 | 23 | 22 | $14

E Village | 433 E. Sixth St. (bet. Ave. A & 1st Ave.) | 212-388-0882 | www.deathandcompany.com

Devotees of "drink couture" "die and go to heaven" at this "hip" East Village speakeasy where the emphasis on the art of "inventive mixology" yields "old-world cocktails with modern twists"; the "neo-Goth" interior reeks of "funereal chic" and the "well-regulated crowd" (thanks to a "no-standing" rule) keeps the "feeling of exclusivity intact" - though the "premium" prices are a killer.

Hotel Delmano

- | - | - | E

Williamsburg | 82 Berry St. (9th St.) | Brooklyn | 718-387-1945

Something "adult" arrives in Williamsburg via this "sexy" new "hipster hideaway" where bartenders in vests and ties stir meticulously concocted cocktails in a "candlelit" space that evokes a "'20s-style" European salon; true, the pops may be pricey, but that's not keeping "arty types" away from this "supertrendy" place.

JakeWalk, The

- | - | - | M

Carroll Gardens | 282 Smith St. (Sackett St.) | Brooklyn | 347-599-0294 | www.thejakewalk.com

Bringing a speakeasy vibe to Smith Street, this new bar/cafe displays a sly sense of humor by naming itself after the unsteady stride caused by bootleg Prohibition booze; in fact, it's a classy joint featuring a long wine list, 120-plus whiskeys, finely made cocktails and small-plate accompaniments, all served by a nattily attired staff.

PDT

27 | 23 | 24 | $13

E Village | 113 St. Marks Pl. (bet. Ave. A & 1st Ave.) | 212-614-0386 | www.pdtnyc.com

Prove "how in-the-know you are" at this "sneaky" speakeasy accessed through a "Maxwell Smart phone booth" in the East Village's Crif Dogs, where "expert mixologists" whip up "imaginative concoctions" in compact, "taxidermy"-adorned digs; the "polite exclusivity" (the name's short for 'Please Don't Tell') is due to a no-standing rule, so reservations are essential - "someone must have told."

Pegu Club

25 | 26 | 23 | $14

SoHo | 77 W. Houston St., 2nd fl. (bet. W. B'way & Wooster St.) | 212-473-7348 | www.peguclub.com

"Chemical engineers are more relaxed about their work" than the "serious" mixologists at Audrey Saunder's "effortlessly hip" SoHo lounge catering to "cocktail connoisseurs" craving a "properly shaken, properly stirred drink" (with an "emphasis on gin"); the recipe for its success consists of "attentive" service, a "sexy", second-floor space that channels "Colonial India" and "expensive", "dangerously tasty" libations that are "tiny" but oh-so-"potent."

GAY/LESBIAN BARS

No explanation necessary

Cattyshack
23 | 17 | 19 | $8

Park Slope | 249 Fourth Ave. (bet. Carroll & President Sts.) | Brooklyn | 718-230-5740 | www.cattyshackbklyn.com

"Just what the ladies ordered", this "amiable" Park Slope lesbian bar allows its "diverse" followers "plenty of prowling space" over "two floors of action", complete with a "lovely rooftop porch" and DJs to "get the crowd excited"; with its "happening theme nights", it's a "purrfect" fit for the neighborhood.

Metropolitan ⊭
∇ 19 | 13 | 18 | $6

Williamsburg | 559 Lorimer St. (bet. Devoe St. & Metropolitan Ave.) | Brooklyn | 718-599-4444

Although known as a "gay hipster" haunt, this Williamsburg "neighborhood" barroom also draws heteros to its "campy cool" quarters done up like an "old general store" (enhanced by "two fireplaces" and a "patio as big as all Brooklyn"); better still, there's "plenty of standing room", the mood's "friendly" and the "bartenders don't skimp on the drinks."

Ritz, The
∇ 20 | 21 | 19 | $13

W 40s | 369 W. 46th St. (bet. 8th & 9th Aves.) | 212-333-2554

Hell's Kitchen's mushrooming gay bar scene continues to swell with the arrival of this "classy" double-decker - on Restaurant Row, no less - offering cocktailing in two cozy bar areas or in two luxe lounges; a killer sound system, buff, "on-point" bartenders and sceney DJs are all part of the package.

Splash ⊭
20 | 15 | 17 | $10

Flatiron | 50 W. 17th St. (bet. 5th & 6th Aves.) | 212-691-0073 | www.splashbar.com

This bi-level Flatiron "mega-gay bar" lures "rainbow crowds" of "bridge-and-tunnel boys" with a great "big" dance floor, "changing theme nights" and "ample eye candy"; despite "expensive" pops and bartenders "hired for their muscles, not their service", it does the trick when you feel like "standing and posing" the night away.

	APPEAL	DECOR	SERVICE	COST

Therapy

APPEAL	DECOR	SERVICE	COST
24	25	21	$10

W 50s | 348 W. 52nd St. (bet. 8th & 9th Aves.) | 212-397-1700 | www.therapy-nyc.com

The "flagship of trendy gay hangouts", this Hell's Kitchen "hot spot" set in a split-level, "woodwork"-heavy setting boasts a "delectable", "tight-tank-topped" staff serving "pricey" drinks "strong enough to make the drag performers look good"; there's "lots to pick from" in the "cute" crowd, so pull up your socks, "suck in your cheeks" and get busy.

Vlada

APPEAL	DECOR	SERVICE	COST
23	20	21	$9

W 50s | 331 W. 51st St. (bet. 8th & 9th Aves.) | 212-974-8030 | www.vladabar.com

"Hot boys" and "icy cold drinks" meet cute at this "trendy" gay duplex that's one of "Hellsea's" "newer cruising grounds"; an "ice"-lined bar (to keep your drinks frosty) and a vlada "homemade" infused vodkas "set it apart" from its competitors, while "cool customers" in the crowd like the "posh" decor.

INTIMATE SETTINGS

Can't-miss destinations to set the mood

Dove, The

APPEAL	DECOR	SERVICE	COST
24	24	21	$10

G Village | 228 Thompson St. (bet. Bleecker & W. 3rd Sts.) | 212-254-1435

An "underground bar" in the "NYU district" that's "not an underground scene", this "cross between a '20s speakeasy and a tearoom" is a "living room" away from home for "intellectual" types who enjoy "conversation"; "lush" sofas, candles and "muted" music set a "romantic hideaway" mood, lubricated by "creative" cocktails.

Flûte

APPEAL	DECOR	SERVICE	COST
22	21	20	$14

Flatiron | 40 E. 20th St. (bet. B'way & Park Ave. S.) | 212-529-7870
W 50s | 205 W. 54th St. (bet. B'way & 7th Ave.) | 212-265-5169
www.flutebar.com

"Bubbly, bubbly everywhere and oh so much to drink" could be the motto of this "swanky" twosome offering an "unrivaled champagne selection" as well as an "extensive" cocktail list; the smallish Midtown original (a former speakeasy) abounds with "dark, intimate" corners that are "cozy for couples, awkward for others", while the high-ceilinged Flatiron outpost is twice as large; either way, "be prepared to spend."

	APPEAL	DECOR	SERVICE	COST
Milk and Honey	27	22	26	$15

LES | 134 Eldridge St. (bet. Broome & Delancey Sts.) | www.mlkhny.com

"Hard to find" and even "harder to get into", this "hush-hush" Lower Eastsider is a "speakeasy in the best sense", accessed "cloak-and-dagger"-style by dialing a "secret phone number" and reserving a booth in advance; the payoff is "superb cocktails" mixed by "hard-working" bartenders, and though it's "becoming less exclusive", "professional drinkers" report this is "still a very special place" indeed.

	APPEAL	DECOR	SERVICE	COST
Shalel Lounge	24	24	16	$10

W 70s | 65½ W. 70th St., downstairs (bet. Columbus Ave. & CPW) | 212-873-2300

There's "no sign" on the street for this "sultry", "subterranean oasis" under an Upper West Side Greek taverna, but the word has gotten out, so the "nooks-and-crannies" setting fills up fast on weekends; "lots of candles", "grottoes" and a "waterfall" add to its "sexy" sheen, and most are so involved in "PDA" that they fail to notice the "poor service."

	APPEAL	DECOR	SERVICE	COST
Temple Bar	24	24	23	$14

NoHo | 332 Lafayette St. (bet. Bleecker & Houston Sts.) | 212-925-4242 | www.templebarnyc.com

"Full of dark corners for dark deeds", this "seductive" NoHo bar is "not a substitute for foreplay, it's foreplay embodied", with a "low noise level", "astute service" and strong, "old-school" cocktails; in short, it works well for a "sexy assignation" with your "secretary" or when rendezvousing with a "double agent."

JAZZ CLUBS & PIANO BARS

A little retro, a little romantic

	APPEAL	DECOR	SERVICE	COST
Birdland	23	19	18	$14

W 40s | 315 W. 44th St. (bet. 8th & 9th Aves.) | 212-581-3080 | www.birdlandjazz.com

Some of the "best" names in "swingin' jazz" land onstage at this "comfortable" Theater District supper club, a "convenient" pick for natives and "out-of-towners" alike; "any table" provides a "decent view", but to avoid "expensive" outlays, the less-well-off may be better off barside.

	APPEAL	DECOR	SERVICE	COST
Blue Note	23	17	17	$15

G Village | 131 W. Third St. (bet. MacDougal St. & 6th Ave.) | 212-475-8592 | www.bluenote.net

See "world-class jazz" masters so "up-close" you'll "be ducking the trombone" at this "famous" Village music club where the "definitive" lineups keep the "funky" space jammed with cognoscenti and "tourists" alike; "stuck-up" service and "exorbitant" prices elicit some "blue notes", but when you're "five feet away from legends", the rest is "incidental."

Brandy's Piano Bar

23 | 14 | 20 | $10

E 80s | 235 E. 84th St. (bet. 2nd & 3rd Aves.) | 212-650-1944 | www.brandysnyc.com

Whether you're coming from "Broadway" or "Nebraska", you'll want to "bust out a tune" at this UES piano bar where the "witty" staff hosts "fabulous" songfests and open-mike nights; it's a "blast" "even if you're not gay", but the "teeny" room "fills up fast", so insiders "arrive early."

Dizzy's Club Coca-Cola

25 | 24 | 21 | $14

W 60s | Time Warner Ctr. | 10 Columbus Circle, 5th fl. (60th St.) | 212-258-9595 | www.jalc.org

"World-class" live jazz, "beautiful acoustics" and "spectacular views" of Central Park combine to put this "intimate" yet "comfortable" berth of the cool at the Time Warner Center miles ahead of other venues; ok, it's "expensive", but "choose the right gig and you're golden" (the "after-hours $10 deal" is an "incredible bargain").

Don't Tell Mama

24 | 16 | 22 | $11

W 40s | 343 W. 46th St. (bet. 8th & 9th Aves.) | 212-757-0788 | www.donttellmamanyc.com

Do "tell mama" (she'll want "to come as well") about this "low-pressure" cabaret/sing-along spot on Restaurant Row, where "hilarious" servers "belt out show tunes" and "Broadway hopefuls" "practice their audition songs" on open-mike night; ok, the vibe may be "hokey" and the shtick "canned", but it's an "absolute blast if you're with the right people."

Le Poisson Rouge

- | - | - | M

G Village | 158 Bleecker St. (bet. Sullivan & Thompson Sts.) | 212-796-0741 | www.lprnyc.com

Carved out of the legendary Village Gate space, this new Greenwich Villager is a self-described 'multimedia art cabaret' offering music, dance and theatrical performances as well as film screenings and special events; an adjoining lounge functions as a cafe by day and a barroom after dark.

Smalls ⊭ 24 | 14 | 16 | $9

W Village | 183 W. 10th St. (7th Ave. S.) | 212-675-5091 | www.fatcatjazz.com

A "teeny club" with a "big heart", this cash-only West Village "treasure" - "completely redone with a bar" and "no longer BYO" - serves up "steamy jazz" till the "crack of dawn" to an "international" "cool-cat" crowd; just remember "if your conversation drowns out the band, you'll suffer the consequences."

JUKEBOXES

Give your evening a soundtrack all its own

Ace Bar 21 | 17 | 17 | $7

E Village | 531 E. Fifth St. (bet. Aves. A & B) | 212-979-8476 | www.acebar.com

Like a "Chuck E. Cheese for the not-so-grown-up", this East Villager offers everything from Skee-Ball to video games plus "cheap brews" in an ample space resembling "your cool friend's basement"; throw in a "rad" collection of "old-school lunchboxes" and it saves everyone from "preppies" to "frat boys" the fare to "Coney Island."

Dark Room 18 | 13 | 16 | $9

LES | 165 Ludlow St. (bet. Houston & Stanton Sts.) | 212-353-0536

Despite - or perhaps because of - its "dim" "dungeon" atmosphere, this subterranean Lower Eastsider has developed a "diverse crowd" of "hipsters", "striped-shirt guys and the women who love them", all "ready to party" ("be prepared to sweat on strangers"); naysayers call the overall feel of "making out in your parents' basement" a negative.

Home Sweet Home 19 | 17 | 16 | $9

LES | 131 Chrystie St., downstairs (bet. Broome & Delancey Sts.) | 212-226-5708

Be it ever so humble, this "subterranean" Lower Eastsider supplies "funky tunes" and "relatively cheap drinks" in a space channeling "your grandfather's old basement", complete with "wacky taxidermy", "oddball artifacts" and beat-up couches for "late-night smooching"; though it's "not for everyone", "total hipsters" say it sure "feels like home."

	APPEAL	DECOR	SERVICE	COST

Magician ⇏ | 16 | 12 | 20 | $6

LES | 118 Rivington St. (Essex St.) | 212-673-7851
There's "minimal" decor at this "blank-canvas" LES barroom, but that doesn't faze the "hipsters" who barrel in for "strong" pops at "cheap" tabs (particularly during "midnight happy hour"); since it's a magnet for local bloggers, you can "get tomorrow's blog entries here tonight."

Marshall Stack | 22 | 18 | 22 | $7

LES | 66 Rivington St. (Allen St.) | 212-228-4667
"Not trashy" but "not too sceney" either, this "tin-ceilinged" LES rock 'n' roller is named for a bank of stage amps but keeps the dial on "mellow" for "laid-back" types with an "array of beers" and "eclectic wines"; it marshals "lots of character", and the "classic jukebox" is way "hot" too.

Mercury Bar | 16 | 14 | 16 | $10

Murray Hill | 493 Third Ave. (bet. 33rd & 34th Sts.) | 212-683-2645
W 40s | 659 Ninth Ave. (46th St.) | 212-262-7755
www.mercurybarnyc.com
"Drunk suits" chase "super-toasted" skirts at the Murray Hill branch of this sports bar duo that's "indistinguishable from all the rest on that stretch of Third Avenue"; "if you'd like to be able to hear anyone speak", try the "more laid-back" Hell's Kitchen edition.

Rusty Knot | - | - | - | M

W Village | 425 West St. (W. 11th St.) | 212-645-5668
Anchored on the West Side Highway, this shipshape new bar grafts a dive (rec-room paneling, racy girlie murals) onto an old-salt's tavern (aquatic taxidermy) and ups the ante with a pool table, a well-curated jukebox, Hudson River sunsets and signature rum-based cocktails served in tiki mugs; given its small dimensions and ultrahip Freemans/ Spotted Pig pedigree, waits at prime times come with the territory.

JUROR-FRIENDLY

Further that new waiting-room bond with a drink invite

Dakota Roadhouse ⇏ | ▽ 15 | 10 | 17 | $8

Financial District | 43 Park Pl. (bet. Church St. & W. B'way) | 212-962-9800 | www.dakotaroadhouse.com
"Quirky", faux-redneck decor supplies the "charm" at this Financial District honky-tonk where guys in ties come to "relax without the

trendy wannabes"; "cheap drinks" and "fried food" supply ample energy for watching sports on the "flat-screens" when not playing pool, darts and foosball.

John Street Bar & Grill

16 | 10 | 17 | $7

Financial District | 17 John St. (bet. B'way & Nassau St.) | 212-349-3278 | www.johnstreet.com

The "market fluctuates", but this Financial District "dive" holds tight with a "grassroots" crowd of "bikers", "construction workers" and random Wall Street "professionals"; maybe the "hole-in-the-wall" decor verges on "dungeon"-like, but it's "cheap", unaffected and open late, a rarity in a "neighborhood that closes early."

Raccoon Lodge

15 | 11 | 18 | $7

Financial District | 59 Warren St. (bet. Church St. & W. B'way) | 212-227-9894

"Still alive after all these years", this "last of the lodges" holed up in the Financial District is a "genuine dive bar" with a "hills-of-West-Virginia" vibe; a pool table and "fairly hot" barmaids add to the "fun", though all the action takes place "after work" - it's "empty after happy hour."

17 Murray

14 | 13 | 18 | $11

Financial District | 17 Murray St. (bet. B'way & Church St.) | 212-608-3900 | www.17murray.com

Pick up all the "political" poop at this Financial District "local", a "popular" caucus for "City Hall" and Centre Street denizens who elect to "defer going home at night"; maybe it's too "isolated" and "lacks atmosphere", but for certain constituencies its "low cost" is enough of a draw.

PHOTO BOOTHS

Document your (love) life story

Dave & Buster's

21 | 17 | 17 | $10

W 40s | 234 W. 42nd St., 3rd fl. (bet. 7th & 8th Aves.) | 646-495-2015 | www.daveandbusters.com

"One chain that fits in nicely" in Times Square, this massive arcade (aka "Chuck E. Cheese for grown-ups") appeals to "thirtysomethings" who like to play "games of chance" with a "joystick in one hand and a beer in the other"; ok, the "blinking, flashing, noisy" scene is "not sophisticated", but "we all have to let our inner child out now and then."

	APPEAL	DECOR	SERVICE	COST
GalleryBar	19	20	17	$10

GalleryBar

LES | 120 Orchard St. (bet. Delancey & Rivington Sts.) | 212-529-2266 | www.gallerybarnyc.com

A daytime gallery with "rotating art", this "cool" Lower Eastsider segues into an "unpretentious" nightspot with a "chill atmosphere" upstairs and "great mixes" from deckmeisters in its subterranean lounge; it may be a tad "mainstream", but it still gets pretty "sweaty on a weekend."

Hugs

∇ 17 | 11 | 17 | $8

Williamsburg | 108 N. Sixth St. (bet. Berry St. & Wythe Ave.) | Brooklyn | 718-599-5959

This "fun" new bar on Williamsburg's North Sixth Street strip features squared-off banquettes and underground DJ sets; games of Skee-Ball and Guitar Hero (plus free Sunday night movies and popcorn) add enough quirky appeal to guarantee that it's "packed on weekends."

Niagara & Lei Bar

19 | 14 | 18 | $7

E Village | 112 Ave. A (7th St.) | 212-420-9517 | www.niagarabar.com

A random "mess of the usual East Villagers" populates this frenetic venue where "punks" share pints with "bankers" in the "crowded" bar; downstairs in the tiki lounge, "sweaty bodies" "bust a move" alongside go-go dancers, while "model wannabes monopolize the photo booth."

Otto's Shrunken Head ⇏

21 | 18 | 16 | $8

E Village | 538 E. 14th St. (bet. Aves. A & B) | 212-228-2240 | www.ottosshrunkenhead.com

"Tiki fantasy meets garage rock" at this random East Village dive where "tacky Polynesian decor" collides with a tattooed hard-rock crowd; it "takes kitsch to a whole new level" with a "metal DJ" in the front bar and live bands in the back room, and after a couple of frozen "sugary drinks", no one cares that "this place doesn't make sense."

ROOFTOPS

Uniquely NY skyline settings

Bookmarks

24 | 22 | 20 | $13

E 40s | Library Hotel | 299 Madison Ave., 14th fl. (41st St.) | 212-983-4500 | www.hospitalityholdings.com

Reminiscent of the (imaginary) "rooftop of your own Manhattan apartment", this "oasis above the Midtown fray" is a "fashionable" alfresco space crowning a "hip hotel", with a slim slate patio, garden furniture and a winter solarium; golly, it's "expensive", but the "tight quarters" are still thronged with "Euro tourists" and other "cosmopolitan" types.

Delancey, The

20 | 21 | 17 | $9

LES | 168 Delancey St. (bet. Attorney & Clinton Sts.) | 212-254-9920 | www.thedelancey.com

"It's all about the all-year-long roof deck" at this LES triplex where the "leafy" alfresco scene comes complete with a view of the Williamsburg Bridge off-ramp; the basement cabaret and main floor barroom have such "different vibes" that you can "go barhopping without leaving the building", but for best results, "bring your own crowd."

Empire Hotel Rooftop

- | - | - | E

W 60s | Empire Hotel | 44 W. 63rd St., 12th fl. (bet. B'way & Columbus Ave.) | 212-956-3313

Bringing some swank to the city's burgeoning rooftop scene, this sprawling new aerie atop the Empire Hotel features two decks equipped with retractable roofs set between a big, glass-enclosed bar; a mammoth vintage neon sign as well as views of Lincoln Center and the Upper West Side make the drinking all the more intoxicating; P.S. get a room to access the guests-only terraces above with private cabanas and a swimming pool.

Highbar

- | - | - | E

W 40s | 251 W. 48th St., 16th fl. (8th Ave.) | 212-229-0010 | www.highba-nyc.com

Hell's Kitchen's latest rooftop, this velvet-ropey newcomer is a sleek double-decker that employs bamboo shoots, tropical plants and Hudson River views to draw its cool-cat crowd; much of the medium-size space is covered, so inclement weather is never a problem here, and there's a totally enclosed downstairs den for VIPs.

Plunge

25 | 23 | 16 | $15

Meatpacking | Gansevoort Hotel | 18 Ninth Ave. (bet. Little W. 12th & 13th Sts.) | 212-206-6700 | www.chinagrillmgt.com

"Bankers looking to spend their bonuses" and "Jersey girls trying to get their attention" collide at this "glam-all-the-way" Meatpacking rooftop/"pool lounge" known for its "incredible" views of Downtown Manhattan and the Hudson; though the pricing is equally "sky-high", the cocktails are the "size of an aquarium" and the staff's "attitude is free", so when you need a break from "navigating cobblestones in stilettos", this one's a "must."

Salon de Ning

APPEAL	DECOR	SERVICE	COST
-	-	-	VE

W 50s | Peninsula Hotel | 700 Fifth Ave., 23rd fl. (55th St.) | 212-903-3097 | www.salondening.com

A slight reworking of the Peninsula Hotel's former Pen-Top bar, this ritzy rooftop offers inspiring Midtown views from its two outdoor terraces and glass-enclosed bar, now redone with a vague 'Shanghai deco' look (think lacquered screens and Chinese daybeds); of course, sky-high tabs come with the lofty territory.

230 Fifth

APPEAL	DECOR	SERVICE	COST
25	23	16	$13

Chelsea | 230 Fifth Ave., penthouse (bet. 26th & 27th Sts.) | 212-725-4300 | www.230-fifth.com

The latest "'it' roof bar", this "sprawling", vaguely "tropical" deck crowning a Chelsea office building is "swamped" with "suity" "mingling singles" marveling at the "awesome cityscape" vistas and disregarding the "snooty service" and "steep" tabs; the "bottlenecked elevators" let out on an indoor penthouse that channels a "cruise-ship disco", but upstairs the "top-of-the-world" scene is the "only place to be during the summer."

TRIVIA NIGHTS

Deflect first-date awkwardness with a little friendly competition

Last Exit

APPEAL	DECOR	SERVICE	COST
20	15	23	$7

Cobble Hill | 136 Atlantic Ave. (bet. Clinton & Henry Sts.) | Brooklyn | 718-222-9198 | www.lastexitbar.com

Cobble Hill's "first hipster bar" sports a "funky living room–ish setting" with "interesting" artwork on the walls and a "low-key" vibe in the air; a "cool" back garden and occasional "dorktastic trivia" contests lead loyalists to label it "one of the best on Atlantic" Avenue.

Pete's Candy Store

APPEAL	DECOR	SERVICE	COST
23	17	20	$7

Williamsburg | 709 Lorimer St. (bet. Frost & Richardson Sts.) | Brooklyn | 718-302-3770 | www.petescandystore.com

"Far enough from Manhattan" that it's "safe from the Manolo Blahnik"-wearers, this "quirky" Williamsburg magnet for the "thinking drunk" is a "delightfully neighborly" nexus with a "beat-up-to-perfection" ambiance; its "biggest draws" are its "game nights" (bingo, scrabble, trivia quizzes, spelling bees) backed up by a "sweet backyard", "generous cocktails" and "loud art music" in a tiny adjacent performance space.

Slipper Room ∇ 20 | 19 | 16 | $8

LES | 167 Orchard St. (Stanton St.) | 212-253-7246 | www.slipperroom.com

There's something "different every night" at this "blast" of a Lower East Side performance space that stages everything from "comedy shows" to "trivia spectaculars" to "hot burlesque"; ok, the "talent varies wildly" and the "acts can drag on", but few in the very "mixed" crowd care - most everyone's "smashed and silly by midnight."

Sound Fix Lounge - | - | - | M

Williamsburg | 110 Bedford Ave. (11th St.) | Brooklyn | 718-388-8087 | www.soundfixrecords.com

Adjacent to Sound Fix Records, this Williamsburg hang has been given a serious makeover, evolving from a coffeehouse into a full-fledged bar and performance venue hosting such high-caliber indie acts as Beirut, Oneida and the Mountain Goats; listening parties, Tuesday night music trivia and other arty events keep the plugged-in clientele coming.

WINE BARS

For an upscale alternative to the usual drinks date

Accademia di Vino 22 | 22 | 20 | $15

E 60s | 1081 Third Ave. (bet. 63rd & 64th Sts.) | 212-888-6333 | www.accademiadivino.com

There's "finally a hit" at this revolving-door Upper Eastsider, an "attractive" space that's been reinvented as an enoteca/trattoria/pizzeria, featuring a "superb wine list" of mostly Italian labels decanted at two separate bars; despite a "few kinks" servicewise, there's "lots of action" for "geriatric and young" types alike at this "much needed" spot.

Bacaro 21 | 22 | 19 | $15

Chinatown | 136 Division St. (bet. Ludlow & Orchard Sts.) | 212-941-5060

Channeling a "classic Venetian wine bar" in Chinatown, this "charming" new offshoot of Peasant is a "rustic jewel" furnished with a marble bartop, "cozy farm tables" and a brick-lined basement grotto that's simply "first date perfection"; it's usually "busy" with "lotsa hotties" sampling "nice" Italian vinos, so waits come with the territory.

Gottino

22 | 22 | 22 | $15

G Village | 52 Greenwich Ave. (bet. Charles & Perry Sts.) | 212-633-2590 | www.gottinonyc.com

"Rustic" yet "civilized", this "terrific" new Village wine bar features a "wonderful" Italian vino selection poured "with a smile" by "professional" staffers in a room resembling a "relaxed" patch of Tuscany; it's already drawing "convivial crowds", but go early, since "seats are few and far between."

Solex

22 | 20 | 21 | $14

E Village | 103 First Ave. (bet. 6th & 7th Sts.) | 212-777-6677

A "sleek" East Village nexus, this "fetching" French wine bar is a "dignified" yet "accessible oasis" where "knowledgeable" sommeliers pour a "lovely selection" of *vins* matched with "delectable finger foods"; the "narrow" setup bounded by "blond woods" and a wavy ceiling is either "claustrophobic" or "cozy", depending on who's talking.

Ten Bells ⇏

- | - | - | M

LES | 247 Broome St. (bet. Ludlow & Orchard Sts.) | 212-228-4450

Named for the British pub where Jack the Ripper picked up his victims, this petite new Lower East Side wine bar lives up to it with a killer list of global organic wines; otherwise, it's a moodily lit space that's drawing the same boho/Euro following as its siblings, Le Père Pinard and Les Enfants Terribles.

Terroir

- | - | - | M

E Village | 413 E. 12th St. (bet. Ave. A & 1st Ave.) | www.wineisterroir.com

A few doors east of its parent, Hearth, lies this new East Village enoteca offering a reasonably priced selection of vinos from around the world accompanied by chef Marco Canora's cured meats and cheeses; the mood is low-key, the setting utilitarian - with a communal table running the length of the smallish space - and its popularity immediate.

WHERE TO BREAK UP

FOOD | DECOR | SERVICE | COST

Restaurants

COMMUTER OASES

For the quick-and-easy getaway after

Cafe Centro ☒ *Mediterranean* 19 | 18 | 19 | $48

E 40s | MetLife Bldg. | 200 Park Ave. (45th St.) | 212-818-1222 | www.patinagroup.com

The "classic business lunch" is in full swing at this "vibrant" brasserie near Grand Central that lures throngs with "dependable" Mediterranean meals, "efficient" service and "commuter convenience"; those seeking "more relaxed", crowd-free dining report that "dinner's a delight."

Capital Grille *Steak* 23 | 22 | 22 | $67

E 40s | 155 E. 42nd St. (bet. Lexington & 3rd Aves.) | 212-953-2000 | www.thecapitalgrille.com

"Suits" say this Grand Central-area chain link "doesn't feel like a chain", but rather is a "capital" place to chow down on "outstanding" cuts of beef with "superb" service that "bucks the gruff" steakhouse norm; few mind paying for the experience.

HK ◐ *American* ▽ 17 | 18 | 17 | $34

Garment District | 523 Ninth Ave. (39th St.) | 212-947-4208 | www.hkhellskitchen.com

A "bright" spot located on an "unremarkable stretch" near the Lincoln Tunnel, this "trendy" American dishes out "fancy comfort food" in "chic", minimalist environs; while the "service could use some fine tuning", the "hip scene", "pretty" patrons and "reasonable" costs are fine as is.

Metrazur ☒ *American* 20 | 21 | 18 | $53

E 40s | Grand Central | East Balcony (42nd St. & Vanderbilt Ave.) | 212-687-4600 | www.charliepalmer.com

"Worth missing your train for", Charlie Palmer's "so NYC" New American in Grand Central Terminal is a "magical place" thanks to its "balcony" seating "overlooking the Concourse"; maybe the overall experience is "expensive" "for what you get", but the "people-watching" is beyond compare.

Metro Marché *French* 19 | 15 | 18 | $36

W 40s | Port Authority | 625 Eighth Ave. (41st St.) | 212-239-1010 | www.metromarche.com

"Who'd of thunk" you'd find a "quality" French brasserie with "reasonable" prices smack in the middle of "seedy Port Authority"?; the "service keeps pace" with the location's "hurried rhythm", and for those with no time to linger there's a "take-out counter" too.

COOL LOOS

Escape to a place more interesting than your companion

Morimoto *Japanese* 25 | 26 | 23 | $80

Chelsea | 88 10th Ave. (bet. 15th & 16th Sts.) | 212-989-8883 | www.morimotonyc.com

Iron Chef Masaharu Morimoto's "signature flair" is on "electrifying" display at this "stunningly cool" West Chelsea Japanese, which presents "phenomenal" cuisine and "discreet" service in a space that's "über-stylish" down to the "high-tech bathrooms"; however, it's a "big-time" "investment", especially if you "go wild" and order omakase.

Schiller's ◐ *Eclectic* 18 | 19 | 17 | $38

LES | 131 Rivington St. (Norfolk St.) | 212-260-4555 | www.schillersny.com

An "über-cool" crowd creates "wall-to-wall buzz" at Keith McNally's LES "Pastis East" dishing up "better-than-you-expect" Eclectic bistro fare paired with "perfect" cocktails; it's best to "be young" here so that you won't mind the "cacophony" and "so-so service."

SEA ◐ *Thai* 21 | 22 | 17 | $27

Williamsburg | 114 N. Sixth St. (Berry St.) | Brooklyn | 718-384-8850 | www.seathairestaurant.com

For "excellent Thai on the cheap", try this "high-energy" Williamsburg venue with a "huge", "nightclub-like" setting complete with a "lotus pond"; "blasting" music, "hit-or-miss" service and "crazy-busy" weekends are part of the deal here.

Tao ◐ *Pan-Asian* 22 | 26 | 19 | $60

E 50s | 42 E. 58th St. (bet. Madison & Park Aves.) | 212-888-2288 | www.taorestaurant.com

With its "loud" "dance music", "jaw-dropping" Zen-themed decor (complete with "giant Buddha") and "lively" "young" clientele, this

Midtown Pan-Asian "feels more like a club" than a restaurant; even though the "pricey" food is "surprisingly good", it's the "electric energy" that the "beautiful" crowd "comes for."

wd-50 ◐ *American/Eclectic* 23 | 18 | 23 | $82

LES | 50 Clinton St. (bet. Rivington & Stanton Sts.) | 212-477-2900 | www.wd-50.com

"Enter with an open mind" and prepare for a "memorable" "adventure" at Wylie Dufresne's highly "experimental" LES New American-Eclectic; it's an "exciting" (some say "wacky") "dinner and science class all in one", but keep in mind that tuition is "high."

DESSERT SPECIALISTS

End things on a sweet note

Cafe Lalo ◐ *Coffeehouse/Dessert* 19 | 19 | 13 | $21

W 80s | 201 W. 83rd St. (bet. Amsterdam Ave. & B'way) | 212-496-6031 | www.cafelalo.com

"Still trading" on its *You've Got Mail* cameo, this "quintessential" UWS dessert dispenser lures "crowds" with a "decadent selection" of "naughty" treats; too bad "indifferent" service, a "touristy scene" and that "cash-only" policy detract from the otherwise "sweet" experience.

ChikaLicious *Dessert* 25 | 17 | 22 | $23

E Village | 203 E. 10th St. (bet. 1st & 2nd Aves.) | 212-995-9511 Ⓜ
E Village | 204 E. 10th St. (bet. 1st & 2nd Aves.) | 212-475-0929 ◐
www.chikalicious.com

"Delectable desserts" are the thing at this "pint-size" East Village sweet specialist offering three-course prix fixes along with optional wine pairings; although it's "pricey for the portion size", the "long lines" out front speak for themselves; N.B. the new across-the-street offshoot doing takeout-only may help curtail the queues.

Chocolate Room, The Ⓜ *Dessert* 25 | 18 | 20 | $17

Cobble Hill | 269 Court St. (bet. Butler & Douglass Sts.) | Brooklyn | 718-246-2600
Park Slope | 86 Fifth Ave. (bet. Prospect Pl. & St. Marks Ave.) | Brooklyn | 718-783-2900
www.thechocolateroombrooklyn.com

"Transcendent chocolate experiences" lie in store at these "heavenly" Brooklyn dessert emporiums (aka "endorphin central") where the "sinful" choices can be paired with wine; still, the "ice-cream parlor" feel and "chipper" service can't shake many out of their "sugar-induced comas."

Kyotofu ◐ M *Dessert/Japanese* 21 | 20 | 20 | $28

W 40s | 705 Ninth Ave. (bet. 48th & 49th Sts.) | 212-974-6012 | www.kyotofu-nyc.com

"Who knew tofu could taste so good?" marvel foodies who fawn over this affordable Japanese Midtowner that "does amazing things with soy", especially in its "luscious" desserts; its sleek, "tight" space is "always full", but the "hip, happening" vibe overcomes all.

Payard Bistro $ *Dessert/French* 23 | 21 | 19 | $54

E 70s | 1032 Lexington Ave. (bet. 73rd & 74th Sts.) | 212-717-5252 | www.payard.com

"Second to none" for "irresistible desserts", François Payard's "picturesque" UES patisserie/French bistro is also "first-rate" for breakfast, "the ultimate ladies' lunch", afternoon tea or an "upscale" dinner; notwithstanding "*très cher*" tabs, most are content to "indulge" in this "taste of Paree" without the plane.

p*ong *Dessert* 22 | 19 | 19 | $57

G Village | 150 W. 10th St. (bet. Greenwich Ave. & Waverly Pl.) | 212-929-0898 | www.p-ong.com

Pastry "genius" Pichet Ong "excels" at this "intimate" Greenwich Village New American, showcasing a "challenging" choice of savory and sweet courses presented as "delightful" small plates; the tasting menus are "the only way to go" here, and though the "grazing" format can "run up the cost", those who visit "expecting the unexpected" can't go wr*ong.

Tailor ◐ M *Dessert* ▽ 23 | 23 | 20 | $66

SoHo | 525 Broome St. (bet. Sullivan & Thompson Sts.) | 212-334-5182 | www.tailornyc.com

"Avant-garde" desserts are the claim to fame of this SoHo New American-Eclectic where wd-50 disciple Sam Mason conjures "one-of-a-kind" dishes both "savory and sweet"; its "far-out" flavors "aren't for everybody", and neither are the "pricey" tabs, but the "smart" vintage-apothecary look and "amazing cocktails" seem to be universal crowd-pleasers.

HOTTEST SERVERS

Ogle, flirt . . . and get a not-so-hot reaction out of your date

Buddakan ◐ *Asian* 23 | 27 | 21 | $63

Chelsea | 75 Ninth Ave. (16th St.) | 212-989-6699 | www.buddakannyc.com

"Putting the awe in awesome", Stephen Starr's "opulent" Chelsea "pleasure dome" features an "impressive" modern Asian menu that nevertheless plays second fiddle to the "glitzy" setting, an "ambitiously staged series of spaces" replete with "incredible chandeliers" and "soaring ceilings"; "steep prices", "loud" noise and "consistent waits" to the contrary, it remains a "New York must" for "the young and hip."

Coffee Shop ◐ *American/Brazilian* 15 | 12 | 12 | $29

Union Sq | 29 Union Sq. W. (16th St.) | 212-243-7969

Food, decor and service are pretty much "afterthoughts" at this "cheap and cheerful" Union Square Brazilian-American best known for its "statuesque" staff and their "who-cares attitude"; "late-night" hours, "sexy" people-watching and "clublike" decibels are all part of the package.

Del Frisco's ◐ *Steak* 25 | 23 | 23 | $72

W 40s | 1221 Sixth Ave. (bet. 48th & 49th Sts.) | 212-575-5129 | www.delfriscos.com

Nirvana for "white-collar alpha males", this "top-flight" Midtown chophouse supplies "gut-busting" slabs of "extraordinary", "buttery" beef in "grand" style; the "spot-on" service and "mahogany-walled" "Texas elegance" make for an "impressive" way to "blow a bundle", though non-expense accounters plug the $39.95 pre-theater menu as a "great buy."

Indochine ◐ *French/Vietnamese* 21 | 21 | 18 | $53

E Village | 430 Lafayette St. (bet. Astor Pl. & 4th St.) | 212-505-5111 | www.indochinenyc.com

Once "impossibly chic" and now simply "classic", this 25-year-old French-Vietnamese near the Public Theater offers "exceptional" dining (and "people-watching") in a setting that's "pretty" to some, but "cheesy" to others; while a few feel it's "lost its mojo", they're easily outvoted year after year.

Pastis ◐ *French* 20 | 20 | 17 | $48

Meatpacking | 9 Ninth Ave. (Little W. 12th St.) | 212-929-4844 | www.pastisny.com

Worth all the "fanfare", Keith McNally's "buzzing" Meatpacking District bistro is "still the place to be" for "delish" French food and a "front-row seat" at a "fabulous" "all-hours" "scene" spanning "trendeez" to "wannabes"; granting the "waits", "madhouse" crowds and servers aspiring "to get discovered", for a "Parisian fix, nobody does it better."

KID CENTRAL

Just keep talking about how much you want to have children, and how soon

Alice's Tea Cup *American* 19 | 20 | 17 | $25

E 60s | 156 E. 64th St. (Lexington Ave.) | 212-486-9200
E 80s | 220 E. 81st St. (bet. 2nd & 3rd Aves.) | 212-734-4832
W 70s | 102 W. 73rd St. (bet. Amsterdam & Columbus Aves.) | 212-799-3006
www.alicesteacup.com

A "fantasy world" for "ladies and little ladies", these "darling" tearooms offer American finger sandwiches, "scrumptious scones" and "giggly chitchat" over an "extravagant assortment" of cuppas; it may be a "madhouse" with "sluggish service" and "ridiculous waits", but ultimately it's "so cute you can't resist."

EJ's Luncheonette ⊄ *American* 16 | 9 | 14 | $22

E 70s | 1271 Third Ave. (73rd St.) | 212-472-0600
W 80s | 447 Amsterdam Ave. (bet. 81st & 82nd Sts.) | 212-873-3444

Ever "crowded" with the "stroller set", this "traditional diner" duo is best known for its "can't-be-beat" breakfasts and "blue-plate specials" piled high with "hearty" "all-American" chow; "no-frills" settings, "ridiculous" weekend waits and a "cash-only" policy are trumped by a "speedy" pace and "good value."

Peanut Butter & Co. *Sandwiches* 19 | 13 | 15 | $13

G Village | 240 Sullivan St. (bet. Bleecker & W. 3rd Sts.) | 212-677-3995 | www.ilovepeanutbutter.com

"If you're a peanut butter lover", "go gourmet" at this Village emporium that "elevates" PB&J "to an art form" with its "creative" sandwiches; it's "pricey" compared with "your grammar school lunchbox", but the results are "too yummy to complain."

Serendipity 3 ◐ *Dessert* 17 | 18 | 13 | $30

E 60s | 225 E. 60th St. (bet. 2nd & 3rd Aves.) | 212-838-3531 | www.serendipity3.com

At this "knickknack"-laden "amusement park" of an Eastsider, "huge, decadent" sundaes and other desserts are dished up for folks on "family outings"; "long, jostling waits" and "arrogant" service are the price for that "ever-popular frozen hot chocolate."

Virgil's Real Barbecue ◐ *BBQ* 20 | 13 | 16 | $34

W 40s | 152 W. 44th St. (bet. B'way & 6th Ave.) | 212-921-9494 | www.virgilsbbq.com

"Yes, you can find" "succulent BBQ" near Times Square at this "barn-like" joint brimming with "tourists and locals" "pigging out" on "affordable" eats and using "towels as napkins"; all in all, it's a "fun, fast, messy" time, even if service blows "hot and cold."

STELLAR VIEWS

Where staring blankly into the distance is considered appropriate

Alma *Mexican* 20 | 21 | 18 | $35

Carroll Gardens | 187 Columbia St., 2nd fl. (Degraw St.) | Brooklyn | 718-643-5400 | www.almarestaurant.com

"Upscale" Mexican grub for "reasonable" dough "justifies the trek" to this "popular" Carroll Gardens cantina with "drop-dead Manhattan skyline views" from its roof deck as a bonus; "iffy service" and "long waits" are blunted by "enormous mojitos" and "killer" margs.

Boathouse *American* 17 | 26 | 17 | $54

E 70s | Central Park | Central Park Lake, enter on E. 72nd St. (Central Park Dr. N.) | 212-517-2233 | www.thecentralparkboathouse.com

Right out of a "Monet painting", this "magical" lakeside New American in Central Park feels like an "elegant country retreat in the heart of Manhattan"; too bad about the "expensive", "catering-hall" food and "somewhat forced" service, but ultimately the "view trumps all" here.

Gigino at Wagner Park *Italian* 20 | 18 | 17 | $43

Financial District | 20 Battery Pl. (West St.) | 212-528-2228 | www.gigino-wagnerpark.com

This Financial District venue with a "reasonably priced" Italian menu is a worthy "sunset" destination given that it has an alfresco patio with "breathtaking" views of the harbor and the Statue of Liberty - you and your dining companion can't help but love it, whatever the mood.

Porter House New York *Steak* 23 | 24 | 23 | $79

W 60s | Time Warner Ctr. | 10 Columbus Circle, 4th fl. (60th St. at B'way) | 212-823-9500 | www.porterhousenewyork.com

The "excellent cuts" from "skilled chef" Michael Lomonaco "melt in your mouth" and the sides are like "comfort food gone to heaven" at this "quiet", "clubby", wood-paneled Time Warner Center steakhouse; enhancing the "elegant", "expense-account" experience are an "impeccable" staff and "divine" fourth-floor views out over Central Park.

Sea Grill ⊠ *Seafood* 24 | 24 | 23 | $67

W 40s | Rockefeller Ctr. | 19 W. 49th St. (bet. 5th & 6th Aves.) | 212-332-7610 | www.theseagrillnyc.com

"Not just for tourists", this "delightful" Rock Center seafooder offers "fabulous" fin fare and "warm hospitality" to go with its "wonderful view" of "the ice rink and Christmas tree in winter"; however, as always, "location" comes at "high cost."

Water's Edge ⊠ *American/Seafood* 22 | 25 | 23 | $65

LIC | East River & 44th Dr. (Vernon Blvd.) | Queens | 718-482-0033 | www.watersedgenyc.com

"Swoon"-worthy views of Midtown, a "formal" setting and "smooth" pro service add up to an "unparalleled romantic evening" at this LIC New American made for "marriage" proposals and "special occasions"; "wonderful" seafood and a free water-taxi to and from Manhattan make the "steep" tab easy to swallow.

VEGETARIAN MENUS

Bring to mind your "picky" eating habits

Angelica Kitchen ⇏ *Vegan/Vegetarian* 20 | 15 | 17 | $26

E Village | 300 E. 12th St. (bet. 1st & 2nd Aves.) | 212-228-2909 | www.angelicakitchen.com

It's "impossible to eat anything unhealthy" at this "creative", cash-only East Village vegan where "earthy" staffers vend "virtuous" vittles "good enough for omnivores"; maybe the "bland" digs need "sprucing up", but the BYO policy helps keep costs low.

Candle Cafe *Vegan/Vegetarian* 23 | 13 | 19 | $32

E 70s | 1307 Third Ave. (bet. 74th & 75th Sts.) | 212-472-0970 | www.candlecafe.com

Vegans and vegetarians are "in their glory" at this "down-home" UES cafe that may be "more casual" and "economical" than its sister, Candle 79, but has food that's "equally good"; indeed, the "fantastic" offerings snuff out complaints of "long waits" and "uninspired decor."

Gobo *Vegan/Vegetarian* 22 | 18 | 18 | $33

E 80s | 1426 Third Ave. (81st St.) | 212-288-5099

G Village | 401 Sixth Ave. (bet. 8th St. & Waverly Pl.) | 212-255-3242

www.goborestaurant.com

Vegan/vegetarian fare "with carnivore appeal" turns up at this "approachable" duo where the "delicious", Asian-accented offerings are both "inventive and virtuous"; tabs are mild, and the chance to "dine with Buddhist monks across from your table" provides an "element of enlightenment" to the meal.

HanGawi *Korean* 24 | 24 | 24 | $46

Murray Hill | 12 E. 32nd St. (bet. 5th & Madison Aves.) | 212-213-0077 | www.hangawirestaurant.com

A "peaceful reprieve from the craziness" of city life, this Murray Hill Korean offers a "unique" vegetarian menu in a "soothing", "shoe-free" environment that recalls a "spa"; "quiet" decibels and "customer-is-king" service help you forget the slightly "expensive" tabs.

Pure Food and Wine *Vegan/Vegetarian* 23 | 22 | 22 | $57

Gramercy | 54 Irving Pl. (bet. 17th & 18th Sts.) | 212-477-1010 | www.purefoodandwine.com

"Awaken your taste buds" at Gramercy's "soothing" stove-free "oasis" that "dispels all notions" of what raw, vegan fare "can be"; its "gorgeous garden" "adds to the sense that mother nature is the maitre d'", though a few cynics quip "why so expensive? - they have no utility bill."

	APPEAL	DECOR	SERVICE	COST

Nightlife

DIVE BARS

Because you're past the point of trying to impress

Billymark's West ⊄

APPEAL	DECOR	SERVICE	COST
15	8	17	$9

Chelsea | 332 Ninth Ave. (29th St.) | 212-629-0118 | www.billymarkswest.com

"Long live the dive bar!" is the rallying cry at this "cheap" West Chelsea "hole-in-the-wall" where darts, pool, video games and "dumpy characters" are the hallmarks of low-rent "perfection"; if you're in the mood for "drinking a lot" and "singing along" with the juke, billy right up.

Ding Dong Lounge

	APPEAL	DECOR	SERVICE	COST
∇	18	16	19	$6

W 100s | 929 Columbus Ave. (bet. 105th & 106th Sts.) | 212-663-2600 | www.dingdonglounge.com

Pleased punks consider this Morningside Heights joint "as slummy as any East Village spot", and that's a compliment from hard-core regulars who value its "old-school music cred", "cheap drinks" and "dark, loud" digs; indeed, the only nonauthentic feature is the "clean bathroom."

Mars Bar ⊄

APPEAL	DECOR	SERVICE	COST
19	11	18	$6

E Village | 25 E. First St. (2nd Ave.) | 212-473-9842

The "roaches wave" when you enter what could be the "most disgusting bar in the city", this East Villager where the "crud on the walls" and "graffiti on the ceiling" keep the "happy drunks" entertained; it's a good place to "work through an existential crisis", just "don't use the bathroom."

Milady's

APPEAL	DECOR	SERVICE	COST
13	6	14	$6

SoHo | 160 Prince St. (Thompson St.) | 212-226-9340

"One of the few hold-out neighborhood dives" in "trendy" SoHo, this "untrendy" barroom with "no atmosphere to speak of" is refreshingly "low-key"; still, foes feel "other than the cheap beer", there's "no reason" to show up given the abundance of "other options" to choose from.

Red Lion

APPEAL	DECOR	SERVICE	COST
19	13	16	$8

G Village | 151 Bleecker St. (Thompson St.) | 212-260-9797 | www.redlionnyc.com

Known for roarin' live music, this Greenwich Village pub follows through with satellite sports that attract random "friends from across the pond"; many say it's among "the best bets on Bleecker", although weekend cover charges are bad news for the "cheap college kids" in the "fun crowd."

Subway Inn ⇏ 17 | 7 | 16 | $6

E 60s | 143 E. 60th St. (Lexington Ave.) | 212-223-8929

"Refreshingly skanky", this 1934 "time capsule" located opposite Bloomingdale's has "all the charm of the subway" with "ripped vinyl seats", a "stale smell" and one of the "worst toilets" in town; the mixed crowd propping up the bar - everyone from "hoodlums" and "bums" to "millionaires" - wonders how it's "survived at such a hot location" for so long but still hopes it "lasts forever."

HOOKAH LOUNGES

End things on a high note

Babel Lounge 21 | 18 | 18 | $11

E Village | 131 Ave. C (8th St.) | 212-505-3468

Have an "authentic" Arabian night at this "cute" Alphabet City Mideasterner where "Moroccan drinks", "hookah pipes" and belly dancing complement the DJ's "pleasing mix" of "international" tracks; boosters babble it's a "real treat", and when the close quarters get "cramped", the patio is a handy way to "escape the heat."

Cloister Cafe 23 | 23 | 15 | $9

E Village | 238 E. Ninth St. (bet. 2nd & 3rd Aves.) | 212-777-9128

At this longtime retreat (since 1977) on a busy East Village block, the lure is a spacious, "romantic" garden with towering trees creating the illusion of seclusion; however, the faux-monastic, stained glass-enhanced interior is "less charming", ditto the so-so service; N.B. heaters allow year-round courtyard seating.

Karma 21 | 18 | 18 | $8

E Village | 51 First Ave. (bet. 3rd & 4th Sts.) | 212-677-3160 | www.karmanyc.com

Those who "still like a smoke with their drink" light up legally at this East Village "hookah den" where an "accommodating" staff will bring you a house water pipe and flavored tobacco, or let you puff from your own pack; it may be "too dark to judge the decor", but the vibe is "cozy" and there are bonus "deep beats in the basement."

	APPEAL	DECOR	SERVICE	COST
Katra	18	21	17	$12

LES | 217 Bowery (bet. Prince & Rivington Sts.) | 212-473-3113 | www.katranyc.com

Hidden in the Bowery's "kitchen supply district", this Moroccan themer (fka Mission) is a stylish, "split-level" lounge/restaurant bedecked with hookahs, latticed nooks and "cushy", pillow-strewn banquettes; there's a "bit of a scene" on weekend nights of the "bridge-and-tunnel" variety.

	APPEAL	DECOR	SERVICE	COST
Kush	22	23	17	$11

LES | 191 Chrystie St. (bet. Rivington & Stanton Sts.) | 212-677-7328 | www.kushlounge.com

Now relocated to "expanded" Lower East Side digs next door to The Box, this "mysterious Moroccan" is a "sensual" spot for digging global DJs while "smoking from some hookahs"; though it's a bit "pricey", romeos report the "Indiana Jones" vibe and kushioned "private" niches are "atmospheric aphrodisiacs."

	APPEAL	DECOR	SERVICE	COST
Le Souk	23	22	17	$11

E Village | 47 Ave. B (bet. 3rd & 4th Sts.) | 212-777-5454 | www.lesoukny.com

Those souking to "sheik all night" settle in at this multilevel East Village restaurant/lounge where the North African theme (think hookahs and belly dancers) convinces most to "get down with their Middle Eastern selves"; alright, it's usually "way too packed" with "all-night waits in line", but the payoffs include a "sexy" vibe, "kicking music" and a party-hearty crowd.

LOUD & CROWDED

It'll be easy to pretend you can't quite hear each other

	APPEAL	DECOR	SERVICE	COST
Home	21	20	17	$13

Chelsea | 532 W. 27th St. (bet. 10th & 11th Aves.) | 212-273-3700 | www.homeguesthouse.com

"Home sweet home" if you "love a scene" (and "look the part"), this West Chelsea bottle service joint draws some hot housemates when it's not serving as a "refugee camp for Bungalow 8 rejects"; the black leather couches and red-lit brick walls make for a "sexy" habitat, but be prepared to "shell out" and brace yourself for "door drama" - unless you "have a beautiful girl on your arm."

Nikki Midtown
21 | 24 | 19 | $13

E 50s | 151 E. 50th St., 3rd fl. (bet. Lexington & 3rd Aves.) | 212-753-1144 | www.nikkimidtown.com

The "beachside" club empire stretching from St. Barths to Sardinia brings "Miami to Midtown" via this "sexy" lounge featuring "dancing on tables", "dining in beds" and "half-naked waitresses sauntering about" in an "all-white, pillow-filled" interior; even though prices are "over the top" and the crowd more "suits" than "St. Tropez", some call it the "best thing to happen to this area since the Waldorf-Astoria."

PS 450
20 | 18 | 18 | $10

Murray Hill | 450 Park Ave. S. (bet. 30th & 31st Sts.) | 212-532-7474 | www.ps450.com

"Young professionals" "get schooled in the art of nightlife" at this "huge", "no-attitude" bar that's become part of the Murray Hill "meat market circuit", populated by "types too cool to go out on Third Avenue"; sure, the "McLounge feel is a turnoff" for some, but it's "always busy", so evidently no one seems to mind much; P.S. insiders whisper the "semi-hidden back room is where it's at."

Sutton Place
18 | 16 | 16 | $9

E 50s | 1015 Second Ave. (bet. 53rd & 54th Sts.) | 212-207-3777 | www.suttonplacenyc.com

Brace yourself for a "boisterous party" at this longtime Midtown triplex, a "male-dominated" scene that draws young "investment banker types" bent on "drowning their work sorrows" (on weekends, it morphs into a "total meat market" that wags tag "Slutton Place"); an "awesome" roof deck is the "main attraction on summer evenings", while the lower floors are pretty "generic" and "personality free."

MEAT MARKETS

With any luck, you'll find a replacement before you head home

Bogart's
14 | 14 | 16 | $11

Murray Hill | 99 Park Ave. S. (39th St.) | 212-922-9244 | www.bogartsonpark.com

Of all the gin joints in the world, Murray Hill's young "suits" turn up at this one "after work" since it's so "convenient" given the lack of options in the 'hood; it's "nothing special", but "management consultants" in a "back-to-college" mood make it their "headquarters."

	APPEAL	DECOR	SERVICE	COST
Brother Jimmy's BBQ	17	13	16	$8

E 70s | 1485 Second Ave. (bet. 77th & 78th Sts.) | 212-288-0999
E 90s | 1644 Third Ave. (92nd St.) | 212-426-2020
Garment District | 416 Eighth Ave. (31st St.) | 212-967-7603
Murray Hill | 181 Lexington Ave. (31st St.) | 212-779-7427
W 80s | 428 Amsterdam Ave. (bet. 80th & 81st Sts.) | 212-501-7515
www.brotherjimmys.com

"Yee-haw!", these "Deep South" themers are a "frat-tastic flashback" to "college days" populated by "red state expats" in "baseball caps and khakis" getting trashed on "PBRs" and "fishbowls of sugary swamp drinks"; sure, they're "immature", but with "ACC sports action", "rockin' '80s" tunes and waitresses "cuter than the Hooters girls", "how can they be bad?"; P.S. a new branch just opened near Penn Station.

	APPEAL	DECOR	SERVICE	COST
Dorrian's Red Hand	16	12	16	$8

E 80s | 1616 Second Ave. (84th St.) | 212-772-6660 |
www.dorrians.com

"Keep your collar up and your morals down" when hitting this "basic" yet "timeless" UES "prep mecca" where "Biff and Muffy's kids" in their "best Waspy duds" gather for "drunken dancing" and "singing to classic rock"; outsiders gripe "beware if you're not blond or blazer-clad."

	APPEAL	DECOR	SERVICE	COST
Mansion	-	-	-	E

Chelsea | 530 W. 28th St. (bet. 10th & 11th Aves.) | 212-629-9000 |
www.mansionnewyork.com

Imported from Miami, this mammoth new ultra-lounge reworks the old Crobar space - and lives up to its name - with tony decor incorporating Persian rugs, crystal chandeliers, book-lined walls and private skyboxes; the former mega-dance floor is gone, remade into a banquetted bottle-service lounge, and there's an art gallery, acrobats and go-go girls galore, and a 20-ft.-tall fireplace to boot.

	APPEAL	DECOR	SERVICE	COST
McFadden's	15	13	15	$8

E 40s | 800 Second Ave. (42nd St.) | 212-986-1515 |
www.mcfaddens42.com

"Life is one big frat party" at this Midtown Irish pub that can get "packed tighter than a woman's suitcase" with the crowds "overflowing onto the sidewalk"; it's such a "total meat market" that you "needn't bother removing your wedding ring", but "watch out or you'll get trampled."

MULTIPLE ENTRANCES/EXITS

Excuse yourself to the bathroom and don't come back

Lucky Jack's

20 | 17 | 21 | $8

LES | 129 Orchard St. (bet. Delancey & Rivington Sts.) | 212-477-6555 | www.luckyjacksnyc.com

Belly up to a "really long" bar that practically "stretches from Orchard to Allen streets" at this "classic" LES Irish pub, a "down-to-earth" joint with absolutely "no pretension"; throw in a pool table and a "nice lounge downstairs", and few are tempted to use the "exits on both ends."

Obivia

24 | 24 | 22 | $12

Little Italy | 201 Lafayette St. (Kenmare St.) | 212-226-4904 | www.obivia.com

A "hot place to go" in suddenly happening Little Italy, this "hip", "Moroccan-themed" bar/lounge is best known for its "schlocky", "old-school pornos" on the "plasma screens" that make for "great conversation starters"; "sexy cocktails" and "comfy couches" make it a worthy destination, no matter the occasion.

OUT-OF-THE-WAY LOCALES

No sense tainting your local favorite

Apothéke

- | - | - | VE

Chinatown | 9 Doyers St. (Bowery) | 212-406-0400

Hidden in an obscure Chinatown alley, this new apothecary-themed bar/lounge (an erstwhile opium den) emits medieval cool via a gold-leafed ceiling, distressed brick walls and a plethora of pharmaceutical paraphernalia; mixologist Albert Trummer offers an encyclopedic drink selection - over 250 specialty cocktails - including his take on the spirit du jour, absinthe; N.B. the unmarked entrance is beneath the Gold Flower Restaurant sign, its previous inhabitant.

40c

▽ 18 | 16 | 19 | $11

E Village | 40 Ave. C (bet. 3rd & 4th Sts.) | 212-466-0800

Bringing some swank to Avenue C, this airy East Village lounge emits a 1940s noir vibe via dim lights and crimson leather booths; the curtained-off niche in the back with a keyhole-shaped entryway (that formerly housed a pool table) has been remade into a space perfect for private parties.

Landmark Tavern
21 | 19 | 20 | $9

W 40s | 626 11th Ave. (46th St.) | 212-247-2562 | www.thelandmarktavern.org

Fortunately, the "charm survived the remodeling" at this born-again "blast from the past" on the far West Side, a "historic" 1868 Irish pub (supposedly "haunted" upstairs) whose "homey", "olde-time" interior "should be on every guided tour of New York"; it's certainly "worth the trek", although it can be "damned difficult to catch a cab home."

Pine Tree Lodge (aka Cabin Club)
24 | 22 | 23 | $7

Murray Hill | 326 E. 35th St. (bet. 1st & 2nd Aves.) | 212-481-5490

"Novelty"-seekers are partial to this "tucked-away", "lodge"-themed bar that "brings the Adirondacks" to Murray Hill and is a "great escape from the 34th Street frat-bar scene"; it also works well for a "reunion with your summer camp buddies", what with the stuffed "dear heads" on the wall, "flannel-covered cushions" and "cool garden patio" out back.

Whistlin' Dixie's Texas Tavern
16 | 16 | 18 | $9

W 50s | 714 11th Ave. (51st St.) | 212-349-4370 | www.dixiestexastavern.com

Settled in the "badlands" of Way West Midtown, this "rollicking" saloon exudes Lone Star kitsch with "frontier" decor, sports-tuned TVs and "accommodating" cowgirls in Stetsons and cutoffs hawking numerous "drink specials"; some sigh "honky-tonk wannabe", but rebels reckon it's "totally trashy fun."

SPOKEN-WORD VENUES

If nothing else, your own words won't be the most perplexing of the evening

Bowery Poetry Club
23 | 19 | 22 | $7

NoHo | 308 Bowery (bet. Bleecker & Houston Sts.) | 212-614-0505 | www.bowerypoetry.com

A "throwback" to "beatnik joints" past, this NoHo art space gives "poets and other performers" a forum to present "the new and the now" while literati "drink, relax" and enjoy "something different"; who knows, the "infusion of culture and counterculture" may even make you "feel young and hip" again.

Cornelia Street Cafe

23 | 17 | 19 | $11

G Village | 29 Cornelia St. (bet. Bleecker & W. 4th Sts.) | 212-989-9319 | www.corneliastreetcafe.com

"Still superior" to many rivals, this "mellow" Village "standby" remains a "charming" venue for dinner and more; its slightly "tight" basement cabaret hosts an eclectic mix of "high art" entertainment ("excellent" folk and jazz, poetry readings and even puppetry), and sidewalk tables are "perfect for sharing some wine" while taking in the passing parade.

Cutting Room

21 | 17 | 18 | $9

Flatiron | 19 W. 24th St. (bet. B'way & 6th Ave.) | 212-691-1900 | www.thecuttingroomnyc.com

Fans dig this casual Flatiron mashup of lounge, restaurant and performance space not only for its comedians, burlesque revivalists and "eclectic" shows by "talented musicians", but also for its "low-key bar" up front; still, some make cutting remarks about "hit-or-miss" programming and caution "don't expect too much" from the "good-looking staff."

Nuyorican Poets Cafe ⇏

21 | 15 | 18 | $7

E Village | 236 E. Third St. (bet. Aves. B & C) | 212-505-8183 | www.nuyorican.org

Its "incredible" Friday night poetry slams may be legendary, but this "entertaining" East Village cafe also stages "progressive" theater, live jazz, stand-up comedy and fierce MC battles; now in its 33rd year, this once-underground haunt hasn't lost its "inclusive" cultural spirit, or thankfully, the "cheap beer."